# The Essence of Lean

## A Superior System of Management

## David Hinds

New Worldview Press

New Worldview Press

editor@newworldviewpress.com

Editors: Larry Alexander and Tyler Tichelaar

Cover design by Luis Hernandez

Production managed by Superior Book Productions

ISBN: 978-0-9975490-0-3

Library of Congress Control Number: 2016918157

Printed in the United States of America

To the love of my life, Brenda,
and to our amazing children, Matthew, Kimberly, and Christopher.

You inspire me and make my life complete.

# Contents

# ACKNOWLEDGMENTS

Since Keith Koenig first welcomed me and our Lean Entrepreneurship students into his distribution center in 2010, I have watched City Furniture undergo a constant stream of startling changes, to the point where it is now a truly iconic example of how successful Lean can be in a non-manufacturing environment. Without Keith's firm belief in the value of Lean and his unwavering commitment to the Lean culture, this success could never have happened.

I am especially grateful to Andrew Koenig who spear-headed the transformation at City Furniture. He has tirelessly worked to advance the Lean cause and "spread the word" by hosting tours. He is a true partner in developing and delivering my Lean Entrepreneurship course, and he is constantly providing help and advice to students after the course is completed. Andrew has proven to be an exemplary Lean leader, and his insight has profoundly influenced the content of this book.

MaryPat Cooper, of Sheridan Healthcare, has been instrumental in building my conceptual understanding of Lean and in demonstrating how effectively Lean can be applied in a large and complex health care organization. Under her leadership, Sheridan has become an outstanding innovator of Lean in health care. MaryPat has been more than generous with her time in working with me and my students as she has allowed us to share in Sheridan's lean journey.

I greatly appreciate the contributions of David Hoyte, President of Transformation Management, for his help in aligning my work with traditional views and methods of Lean. David's extensive contributions included many practical examples from his experiences as an executive leader of Lean initiatives in manufacturing, private equity, and consulting.

Joseph Imperato, Jr. and Joseph Imperato, Sr. of XSolutions Consulting Services, have been long-time beta testers of the 7-step method, and I am most grateful to them for their encouragement and for letting me report on their kaizen event in Chapter 12 of this book. Dr. Jeffrey Liker offered insightful perspectives on the role of waste and the importance of practical scientific thinking. Other individuals who have reviewed drafts of this book and have provided invaluable feedback are Joseph Berenbaum, Dr. Steven Borchert, Ernesto Custodio, Joseph Linksman, and Henry Woodman.

At Nova Southeastern University, I must thank Dr. J. Preston Jones and Dr. Thomas Tworoger of the H. Wayne Huizenga College of Business and Entrepreneurship, for creating an open and entrepreneurial environment in which I could build this model of Lean in parallel with developing and teaching my Lean Entrepreneurship course. Key academic colleagues at NSU who contributed important perspectives and connections with academic theories included Dr. Steven Kramer, Dr. Kimberly Deranek, Dr. Arthur Weinstein, and Dr. Ryan Miller.

I wish to thank the hundreds of graduate students in my classes who have provided so much feedback and inspiration in helping me to shape this book. A number of these students have taken positions as process improvement leaders and facilitators or have built their companies using Lean principles. I am also very grateful to the many entrepreneurs and executives who have opened their organizations to our students. Key host executives included Ted Drum, Bob Gass, Rob and Kevin Kornahrens, Henrik and Kim Laursen, Carlos Rives, and Susan Stanley. I especially want to thank Mike Grimmé of AMC Liquidators, Dr. Robert Coppola of South Florida Vision, and Keith Costello of First Green Bank for their enthusiastic support of Lean and for hosting so many student projects.

In my personal life, I have been incredibly fortunate to have wonderful parents, Richard and Lillian, who taught me the importance of accountability and integrity, showed me how to love, and instilled in me a firm belief in the value of others. My brother Rich showed me just how much can be accomplished if you deeply care about what you do, and my brother Garry has been a constant source of guidance and encouragement throughout my entire life. I am indebted to James Britt, my father-in-law, for his invaluable mentorship, as well as the rest of the Britt family for inspiring me with their entrepreneurial spirit.

I have been blessed with fantastic children, Matt, Kim, and Chris, and their beautiful spouses, Joe and Adri, who have taught me so much about personal character. Our precious grandchildren, Lily, Ben, and Maddie, will certainly grow up to be Lean! However, the luckiest day in my life was the day I met Brenda, my wife and lifelong partner. Her energy, commitment, and acumen as vice president and co-owner of our business ensured the success of our company. Her suggestions and reality checks have been essential in shaping my thinking. Her deep and unwavering love for me, our family, and for those around us whom we hold dear has created a radiant atmosphere of warmth and security. Brenda passionately cares about all the important things in life. She is a truly extraordinary woman, and I will love her forever!

# FOREWORD

WE AT CITY Furniture would have been better off if David Hinds' book, *The Essence of Lean*, were written before we started our pursuit of Lean. And it can help you if you are considering starting or are on a Lean journey. David's new book shares real Lean thinking in practical and easy to understand ways that can be important to any organization or company, especially those *not* in manufacturing.

After spending forty years in building Waterbed City and then City Furniture, I have come to realize that Lean is what I have been looking for my whole life. We started on our Lean journey in 2007 after my son, Andrew, pushed me to learn and read books about Toyota. The Great Recession was going on, and I told him we were busy, but fortunately, he persisted and opened my eyes to a better way—Lean.

We gained the insight that Lean could improve our management system and help us run our business better. However, we faced one major challenge—Lean literature focused almost exclusively on manufacturing and the processes and problem solving related to making products. Few books discussed anything other than manufacturing and none were about retail. Even Toyota had not brought Lean thinking to its car showrooms or the selling process. But all the books theorized that Lean could help any business or organization eliminate waste. That, we have learned, is absolutely true.

David nailed the key issue—Lean will only work well in companies where the culture is aligned to the values of accountability, integrity, respectfulness, and trustfulness. Our first Lean consultant rightfully only agreed to work with us after meeting with our associates and studying our culture. The consultant found that we had a culture where Lean thinking could take hold and grow. Had we been a top-down, autocratic organization, the consultant would have passed on the assignment, knowing Lean would not be successful. In those types of organizations, problems are hidden and blame is feared. In true Lean companies (and we have a long, long way to go to become truly Lean), problems are sought out and exposing them is encouraged as they present opportunities to improve. The culture that is required for people to expose problems openly must be respectful and transparent.

We have found success in blending Lean with a leadership development program that emphasizes celebrating the human spirit and sharing respect and appreciation for our associates in ways that allow our Lean culture to grow and flourish. And it is critical that the leaders of the company live those values. Otherwise, associates will see Lean as an effort to squeeze out labor costs, reduce head count, and improve efficiency without regard for people.

Company leaders need to read about and study Lean principles and methods. However, most people learn best by "doing" Lean, participating in problem-solving kaizens and then continuing to practice Lean as part of their daily routine. That is what Lean is really about, and David scores that idea by sharing that all team members can, and need to be, involved in Lean events.

At City Furniture, Lean started in our distribution center and in our delivery processes, but it has grown into all aspects of our business with countless Lean events. We have brought Lean to our retail sales processes with many kaizens, including one that changed how we greet every guest who enters our showrooms. We brought Lean to our IT team by changing our software development process. We brought Lean to human resources in recruiting and training practices. Lean has had a huge effect on our customer service team, too. It is taking hold in merchandising and marketing, as well. And by "doing" Lean, our associates have learned what Lean really is.

Ask most business people what Lean is and they generally don't know. I call Lean the best management system in the world, and David Hinds has added an important book to support the advancement of that system.

Keith Koenig,

CEO, City Furniture


Dr. David Hinds' book, *The Essence of Lean*, provides an insightful look into what it takes to create a culture of continuous improvement. Speaking from direct and daily experience while working hard to implement Lean within our company of 1,300 associates for the past ten years, I feel this book captures the blood, sweat, tears, failures, and successes that we have experienced throughout our Lean journey. I wish I would have had such a book to help guide me sooner on our path toward becoming truly Lean. I believe every business manager thinks at one point in his or her career, "Is there a better way to manage?" My answer to that is "Yes, there is," and the outline of that management system is in this book. Enjoy!

Andrew Koenig,

Vice President, City Furniture

# PREFACE

A GREAT MANY books have been written on the subject of Lean. Most of these books describe Lean as an extension of the Toyota Production System, which spurred Toyota to expand from a tiny car company after World War II into one of the largest and most successful organizations in the world. As it moved beyond Toyota, Lean essentially transformed the manufacturing industry to the point where now more than 90 percent of manufacturers report using some form of Lean.

Lean is now advancing into health care and is beginning to have an effect on the delivery of medical services. Average wait times in emergency departments have been reduced, and changes are now being seen in a wide variety of hospital departments and other health care applications. Hospitals with Lean programs are reporting substantial improvements in patient satisfaction and safety, productivity, and lead times.

Lean has also made modest inroads into retail and governmental organizations. However, Lean's effect remains largely limited to manufacturing and health care, with the majority of improvements being made by large manufacturers like Toyota. Organizations employing the other 80 percent of the workforce outside of manufacturing and health care are largely unaware of Lean, and few have benefited from this powerful management system.

With the goal of raising awareness and encouraging consideration of Lean principles among this "other 80 percent," this book depicts a unique systems model that presents Lean's essential elements from an overall management perspective. The model described herein is based on general principles of management, operations, and human behavior, revealing important insights into how and why the Lean system works as well as it does. The system reflects two principles of work focusing on waste and flow, and two principles of leadership emphasizing bottom-up management and trust and respect.

Using everyday language and business concepts, this book describes how these Lean system principles can be applied through organizational practices that are not unique to any particular type or size of organization. These practices are presented without resorting to manufacturing terms or examples, which makes it easier for non-manufacturing readers to clearly understand the nature and mechanics of Lean and to imagine how a Lean system could be applied to their own organizations.

Lean is described as a blend of method and culture. The method provides tools and techniques for continuously learning about how to better produce value for your customers and for your organization. The culture is essentially a way of treating employees with trust and respect that makes them *want* to be a part of the system. What is most exciting is recognizing how the method and the culture, when working together in harmony, can produce outstanding organizational performance while at the same time leading to a fulfilling and sometimes even joyful workplace!

For **small and medium-size businesses**, Lean offers an overall template for how to run a business and can provide an invaluable competitive advantage. The Lean system can be scaled down for even the smallest of companies, and implementing Lean in an early stage of an organization's development allows the business to grow around Lean culture and practices without forcing a Lean transformation later on.

In *service industries* where the role of the frontline employee is so critical in providing high quality customer service, a Lean culture fosters higher energy levels and enduring commitment among employees. Because Lean leverages the knowledge and common sense of the people doing the work, it is less dependent on data and can be very effective in dynamic service environments where reliable measurements may be hard to come by.

In *governmental operations*, Lean offers a captivating vision of improvement and the pursuit of perfection, which can substitute for the profit motive. For local, state, and federal government employees who sincerely wish to serve the public in the most efficient and effective way but find themselves constantly "fighting the system," Lean provides a practical framework for waste reduction and process improvement.

For *non-profit organizations,* Lean's goal of eliminating waste and producing value leads to the delivery of higher quality services at lower total cost. This higher productivity level not only leverages existing charitable contributions, it also expands the contributor base by making the organization a more attractive target for future donations.

This book introduces the Lean system to corporate executives and directors, entrepreneurs and business managers, and elected officials and government administrators. It is especially directed toward leaders who are not familiar with Lean but who are actively seeking out new ways of strengthening and growing their organization. While it is not meant to be a comprehensive study, this book does provide sufficient guidance, tools, and techniques to get started on a Lean path.

Part One provides an overview of the Lean system model and what's involved in applying the model to an organization. In Chapter 1, the motivation and methods used in developing the model are discussed. Chapter 2 presents an overview of the complete Lean system and its powerful effects on organizational performance. Chapter 3 explains what it takes to implement the three components of a Lean system, which include method, surface culture, and deep culture.

Part Two presents a more in-depth view of the method component of the Lean system and the Lean principles of waste and flow that support the continuous learning method. Chapters 4 through 7 cover the practices needed to implement these two principles, including standardizing and visualizing a process, assessing value, identifying waste, creating a future vision, and improving flow.

Part Three describes Lean culture and the Lean principles of bottom-up management and trust and respect. Chapter 8 describes the surface culture component of the Lean system and the types of management practices needed to support a bottom-up approach. The importance of trust and respect and the deep culture component are discussed in Chapter 9. Chapter 10 describes the significance of Lean values and personal character in building a strong Lean culture. Lastly, Chapter 11 explores the role of the Lean leader in building and sustaining a Lean system.

In Part Four, Chapter 12 contains instructions and tools for applying the Lean method during a 3 to 5 day event. While the Lean method can be applied in many different ways, this is a well-tested approach that has been quite effective in the hands of leaders and associates who are making a first attempt at Lean improvement. This is the "how-to" part of the book, which can be used to start your own Lean journey as you "learn by doing." Chapter 13 contains some suggestions for follow-up reading in support of your Lean journey.

# PART ONE
# OVERVIEW

# Chapter 1

# In Search of Lean

"There's a way to do it better—find it."
— Thomas A. Edison

### *Is There a Better Way?*

I HAVE ALWAYS been fascinated by the various ways in which an organization can be run. There are so many different methods, techniques, structures, and approaches, I have wondered whether there might be a "better way" to do it, or is the answer simply, "It depends."

Of course, I have seen many management fads come and go, and any experienced leader will tell you that every situation is somewhat different and that there are no magic bullets. However, I have always believed there may be some type of approach that is *generally* better than the others—an approach that could consistently provide superior results regardless of the organization's type or size.

These were burning issues for me after acquiring a faltering whole-sale distribution business in 1988. Faced with rapidly declining sales and serious employee problems, I had to do *something*. After struggling for a few years, I learned that a few distributors were following a program called "Total Quality Management (TQM)." The program emphasized customer focus, continuous improvement, and employee involvement. I especially liked the idea of employee involvement because I always believed that the right frontline employees could be a great source of know-how and energy.

I adopted the philosophy of TQM and combined it with industrial engineering techniques such as process flowcharting and work simplification. I worked with my employees to identify problems and make incremental improvements, asking each day how we could make our company a little bit better than the day before. After our core management team was established, I began to see how this approach was leading us to form strong bonds with our employees, our customers, and our key suppliers. The process management tools that we used were relatively simple and intuitive, and yet they were very effective in our employees' hands.

We learned more and more about our customers, what they really wanted, and how we could best serve their needs. We steadily grew our business and our performance drastically improved. We ultimately took the company from near-bankruptcy to one of the most profitable and respected building supply distributors in the country.

After selling the company and retiring from a thirty-year career in industry and government, I earned a doctoral degree to pursue a further career in academia. This was a great opportunity for me to reflect on and share my leadership experiences while continuing to search for a "better way."

I began to investigate programs such as Lean and Six Sigma. I could see that Lean manufacturing had transformed the way that goods were produced, becoming the standard for production with 90 percent of all manufacturers using some type of Lean method. The doubling of productivity within the manufacturing sector over the past twenty years had no doubt been strongly influenced by the powerful effect of Lean manufacturing methods.

Lean was also beginning to have a noticeable effect on the health care industry. More and more hospitals and other service providers were reporting the use of Lean to provide a new focus on patients' needs. Driven by the overwhelming need for cost reduction and outcome improvement, Lean health care was attracting a great deal of attention and resources.

I was impressed to hear of Lean's effectiveness in improving organizational performance. Lean was reported to improve speed, quality, reliability, productivity, agility, and responsiveness to customer needs, all in a way that improves the working environment and employee satisfaction, resulting in high retention rates for both employees and customers. Commonly reported effects of Lean included the doubling of labor productivity, 90 percent reductions in cycle times, 90 percent reductions in inventory levels, 50 percent reductions in space requirements, and 50 percent improvements in error rates. It seemed as if Lean could possibly be this better way that I was searching for.

### The Best Kept Secret

After studying Lean organizations and realizing that we actually used many elements of Lean in my own distribution business, I decided to develop and teach a graduate MBA course in entrepreneurial management from a Lean perspective. Using Lean as a framework for the course was very useful because it covered both the technical/operational aspects and the managerial/cultural aspects of running and growing a business.

Most of my students were working professionals who came from a variety of industries. What was most curious about these students was that the great majority of them were not even aware of Lean when they entered my class—it seemed as if Lean was being kept a secret! I came to realize that, while Lean *was* being applied outside of manufacturing, these cases were actually quite rare and most published examples were limited to large corporations. I had to ask myself, "Why?" Was Lean something that only applied to manufacturing?

In reflecting on my own experience with TQM and process improvement, I could see the close resemblance between my approach and Lean. Even though examples were uncommon, Lean *was* being used in health care and in other industries such as retail, wholesale, hospitality, education, financial services, and government. I noticed that many organizations like my own had already discovered the benefits of a Lean-style culture, even though they were not aware of the Lean method itself.

Clearly, Lean was not limited to manufacturing. This was not merely a teaching issue—it was a huge untapped opportunity. While Lean was dominating the world of manufacturing and was beginning to transform health care, Lean was still largely unknown among organizations that employ the remaining 80 percent of workers in the U.S. economy! I set out to understand why this was so and what could be done about it.

As I learned more about Lean, I realized there were various factors that concealed this tremendous opportunity. For one thing, the great majority of Lean literature and training was built around the experiences of Toyota as it developed and applied its Toyota Production System. Unfortunately, individuals who were not in manufacturing found it difficult to relate to this work. Leaders in other sectors saw Lean as a specialized program that did not apply to their organization. Entrepreneurs who owned small- or medium-size businesses were especially disappointed because the vast majority of Lean cases were reported in large companies.

Understanding the essential nature of Lean was also difficult. Lean seemed to suffer from an identity crisis. What exactly is Lean? The definitions of Lean vary from one book to another, with each consultant having his or her own view and each organization building its own "house." A brief look at the current Wikipedia page for "Lean" (Lean 2016) shows many different meanings for Lean in business, including a type of thinking, a set of manufacturing principles, a process improvement discipline, and a way of starting a company. McKinsey authors Duncan and Ritter (2014) refer to Lean as an idea, calling it: "One of the biggest management ideas of the past fifty years."

Further confusing the situation are the many different ways in which the term "lean" is used in business. One major problem involves the ambiguous relationship between Lean and Six Sigma, especially with regard to programs that are now commonly called "Lean Six Sigma." To complicate matters, we are now seeing the emergence of something called "Lean Startup"—is that the same as Lean? More confusion arises because of the notion that business should be "lean and mean."

### A Model of Lean

In order to expand awareness and improve understanding, I felt that we needed a clear and generalized description or "model" of Lean. We needed a model that explained the true essence of Lean in a way that would be transferrable and accessible to a broad range of types and sizes of organizations. To do this, the model could not be built around specific problems or points of view associated with Toyota in particular or manufacturing in general.

I began to build such a model. Rather than being a survey of Lean organizations, the model was intended to be a synthesis of what is written about Lean, what theory says about it, and especially how Lean is actually practiced. My frame of reference was to explore whether or not Lean was truly a better way for any type of organization. I sorted through the many different organization-specific descriptions and problems reported in the

Lean literature in order to identify the true *heart of Lean*—the essential elements that are most important in driving performance. In some respects, I wanted to know the lowest common denominator of Lean.

So that I could gain the broadest possible perspective, I looked for Lean ideas in organizations and literature that did not reference the name "Lean" but whose approach seemed similar to Lean. This included companies like Menlo Innovations (Sheridan 2013), which saw corporate culture as a key strategic advantage. Also important and relevant was the emerging literature on trust and respect in organizations.

In addition to describing the "what," I also wanted to know the "how" and the "why" of Lean. Looking for the fundamental principles upon which Lean was built, I needed to explain exactly how and why Lean worked as well as it did. To do this, I considered the insights and perspectives provided by relevant academic theories of management, operations, psychology, and organizational science. However, this was not intended to be a rigorous academic study. My goal was clearly focused on providing a general management model that could be used by my students and by other practitioners.

In building the model, I worked intensively with Lean practitioners, consultants, and educators. I carried out extensive field work with prominent Lean organizations such as City Furniture and Sheridan Healthcare. My greatest inspiration came from Keith and Andrew Koenig of City Furniture who relied on Lean to weather the Great Recession, leading to their emergence as one of the most successful examples of Lean in "the other 80 percent" of the U.S. economy.

### The Crucible

During the six years of model development, I obtained extensive input and reviews from my Lean practitioner partners as well as successful organizations who knew nothing about Lean. I read the Lean literature and attended conferences. I assessed the extent to which the model was consistent with the findings of Collins' landmark study of top companies as reported in his book, *Good to Great* (Collins 2001). I also reflected on the model through the filter of my own hands-on experience with a Lean approach and, more generally, my thirty years of professional and leadership experience in business and government.

I tested the model in the classroom with hundreds of working professional students. Each class involved intensive Lean consulting projects in which students learned and applied the model toward the improvement of processes in real world organizations. These projects represented field tests in a wide range of organizations, including retail, wholesale, hospitality, manufacturing, banking, health care, construction, professional services, education, software, and non-profit organizations.

The model that emerged from this work describes the essential nature of Lean as a system built upon certain principles and practices of process improvement and organizational management. It clearly distinguishes Lean from Six Sigma and other programs. The model has been broadly accepted by Lean practitioners and is consistent with the work of Collins (2001) with regard to Level 5 leaders. In my classes, the model has been learned and applied in a matter of weeks, resulting in a great many success stories, excited students, and satisfied host organizations.

Reflecting on the essential elements of Lean as a system, understanding the general principles upon which it is built, and connecting it with well-accepted theories of operations and management led to an understanding of exactly how and why Lean can be so effective. Recognizing Lean as a general system of management makes it clear that Lean is *not* just for manufacturing and that it *can be applied* to virtually any type or size of organization.

# Chapter 2

# The Essential Lean System

"Engaging the hearts, minds, and hands of talent
is the most sustainable source of competitive advantage."
— Greg Harris, CEO of Quantum Workplace

LEAN IS A vision of how to do work and how to treat people. From the perspective of organizational leaders, Lean is how we run our organization. It is how we deploy our people, processes, and technology toward the accomplishment of our goals. From the perspective of employees, Lean is how we do things and how we work together every day. It is a vision of what we believe in and what we strive for.

As seen on Figure 1, Lean is essentially a system of management in which method and culture are blended together. The method involves a *continuous learning* cycle in which work is standardized and visualized, value and performance are assessed, problems are identified, an ideal process is envisioned, and work is improved in pursuit of that vision.

These work improvement practices are carried out within a *people-driven* culture in which leaders facilitate and guide the work rather than commanding and controlling workers. This type of culture is distinguished by bottom-up management practices such as goal-setting, empowering, partnering, and coaching, and is driven by people whose character reflects the values of accountability, integrity, respectfulness, and trustfulness. These practices and values build strong bonds of mutual trust and respect at a personal level, leading to engagement and transparency at an organizational level.

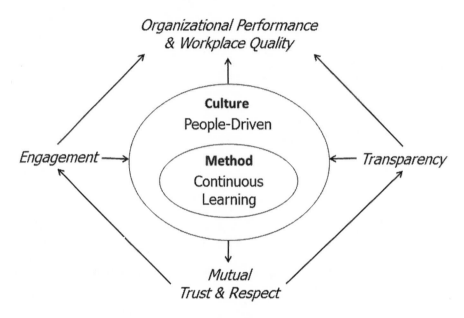

Figure 1. The Essential Lean System

While the method and the culture are both powerful in their own right, it is their integration into a single, cohesive system that produces truly outstanding results. The method directly influences work performance while the culture has broad effects on both organizational performance and employee satisfaction. This translates into higher quality products and services, greater speed and agility, higher productivity, lower cost, and a safer, more fulfilling, and even joyful workplace. This naturally leads to more satisfied and loyal customers and contributes to the sustained growth and profitability of the Lean organization.

## Lean Method

> "Excellent firms don't believe in excellence,
> only in constant improvement and constant change."
>
> — Tom Peters

Process improvement methods are often described as "continuous improvement." In some organizations this means there is always an improvement project going on somewhere. In a Lean organization, continuous improvement means that the method is the way in which the work is actually performed, controlled, and improved on a day-to-day basis. In essence, the Lean method becomes *a way of life.*[1]

With the Lean method, the idea is not to conduct expert-driven studies in order to seek out the "best solution." Rather, employees are constantly looking for small, incremental changes that, over time, add up to major improvements. Sometimes a problem is corrected "on the job" as soon as it is detected. At other times, a more in-depth Lean event may be conducted in which the people doing the work are assembled as a "kaizen team" (See Chair Assembly Kaizen below).

This incremental approach not only leads to improvement, it also builds the knowledge and experience base of employees, which is among the most important assets of an organization. Making small changes and observing the effect on the organization is basically a controlled scientific method and provides the foundation for continuous learning.

In order to enable continuous learning by all employees, the tools are not generally analytical but are relatively simple and visual. While the method certainly incorporates quantitative data, it is not

---

1    Think of an improvement project as "going on a diet" and the Lean method as "good eating habits."

Chair Assembly Kaizen at City Furniture
Keith Koenig, CEO

Early on in our Lean journey, we hired a consultant who got us started on conducting kaizen events, where kaizen means "small change for the better." A kaizen team is basically a group of people who do the work, with at least one person who understands Lean principles who can guide them through the event intelligently. And in a period of time, they reorganize whatever the work is.

One of our first kaizen events was applied in the chair assembly department. Our overseas plant manufactured parts for dining room chairs and then shipped them to the South Florida distribution center for assembly and sale. The process for assembling chairs was relatively simple and similar to the do-it-yourself assembly of furniture and toys that many of us parents are all too familiar with.

A few years before the event, the process had been carefully designed by an engineer from one of the top U.S. engineering schools. So it was the "smartest guy in the room" who laid out the process. Actually, the process seemed to be going quite well and many visitors touring the center from other furniture companies commented, "That was about the best we've seen."

In a one week kaizen event with the people who do the work every day, no engineers, and one Lean consultant, they made a series of changes to the process which more than doubled productivity. And what do you think the people in that group were saying about it? "Hey, that was my idea!"

dependent on that data. Rather, it is dependent upon facts,[2] observations, and common sense that result from the employees' direct participation.

The philosophy that drives the Lean method is that *you should only do things that your customer cares about*. In carrying out this philosophy, all efforts are directed toward producing value for customers and away from producing waste which is of no value to customers.

Waste is a fundamental concept within the Lean method. It is the basis for the first Lean principle, which can be stated as follows:

Lean Principle #1: Waste

*Work processes are most effectively improved by eliminating waste. Waste is the problem.*

In the Lean method, we consider waste to be any activity that does not produce value for the customer and other process stakeholders. Here, waste is not limited to the common definition as something that needs to be discarded. Rather, waste is defined in a broader sense that incorporates defects, waiting, excessive production, excessive inventory, and non-productive activities such as excessive walking, processing, and transportation.

Eliminating waste will lead to a condition of "flow," which is a pattern of smooth and continuous work that proceeds without interruption. Flow is essentially the absence of waste. The concept of flow provides a vision of what the work would look like without any waste. Thus, flow provides a kind of design objective or guiding light that can be used in developing work improvements.

---

2    "Facts" can be thought of as observations of reality that may or may not be supported by data.

This leads to the second Lean principle, which can be stated as follows:

Lean Principle #2: Flow

*Flow is the vision of an ideal work process. Improving*
*flow reduces waste.*

The Lean method is implemented through a series of practices focusing on improving and managing work as illustrated on Figure 2. On the figure, practices are shown as a logical cycle of activity leading to continuous learning. However, these practices may be applied in different sequences and in different ways. For example, a kaizen team will sometimes apply the practices more formally as part of a kaizen event.[3] At other times, an individual employee will simply recognize waste and come up with an improvement "on the spot" as part of his or her daily work.

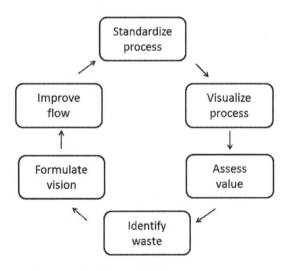

Figure 2. Practices of Continuous Learning

---

3    Refer to Chapter 8, Partnering.

The cycle begins (and ends) with standardizing a "process," which is a stream of activities that produces value for the customer and for the organization. Standardizing a process involves developing "standard work," which is the single best way currently known for carrying out the process. Standard work is documented and can be used by any employee performing the work. Documentation is also important because it ensures that any previous improvements have been captured and can be used, along with the current best practice, as the basis for further learning and improvement, allowing each employee the opportunity to come up with something even better.

The next practice involves visualizing the process itself. Visualization is a key practice in the Lean method because it enables direct observation by all employees leading to identifying waste, making improvements, and sustaining those improvements. A process can be visualized on a process map or "value stream map," which helps a team of employees to share and build their understanding of how the process actually works. The actual implementation of a work process is supported by "visual controls," which indicate the current status and performance of that process.

The type of value that defines a high quality process must then be assessed. This involves identifying the process stakeholders' needs and perceptions in terms of quality, speed, productivity, and compliance. These value perceptions are used as criteria for gauging the current process performance and for creating a vision of what an ideal process would look like. We sometimes assume that we understand our customers when in fact we don't. This practice ensures that we explicitly identify our customers' needs and desires, whether they are external or internal customers.[4]

---

4    An external customer is the paying customer while an internal customer is an employee who uses the output of a particular process.

Identifying waste is an important practice in the Lean method because waste is viewed as the problem. Why create waste when you can create value? Finding the waste can be difficult because we become accustomed to waste as our normal way of doing business. Once waste is recognized, its root cause can be identified, where "root cause" is a controllable factor that causes the waste. Identifying the root cause will lead directly to an improvement because removing the root cause naturally reduces or eliminates the waste.

The next practice is to formulate a Lean vision of the improved process. This vision is an image of how the process might look if it had little or no waste at all and exhibited greatly improved flow that fully satisfied the needs of customers and other stakeholders. This type of vision can be somewhat abstract and is sometimes represented on a "future value stream map." The Lean vision provides employees with direction and presents a challenge as they learn how to move toward the vision by experimenting with small changes to the process.

The final practice of the Lean method involves improving the process flow through a cyclical trial and error approach in which process improvements are identified, evaluated, validated, and implemented (leading to their standardization). These improvements may be significant, although they are often simple changes designed to reduce waste and increase the production of value for customers and process stakeholders. Work that flows will produce higher quality outputs (fewer defects waste), in less time (less waiting waste), with fewer resources (less inventory and non-productive activity waste).

These practices can be implemented in many different ways, and the actual use of tools and activities will vary greatly depending upon the specific needs and resources of each particular organization, as well as its stage of Lean maturity. Organized events are commonly used by early-stage Lean organizations, while mature Lean organizations build continuous learning practices into their regular daily routines and only use events for making significant changes like workplace rearrangement.

The continuous learning practices of the Lean method and the tools commonly used are covered in more detail in Chapters 4 through 7. In addition, instructions for a 7-step method for organizing a Lean event are presented in Chapter 12. This 7-step method should be viewed as an outline or starting point. Over time, you will not only learn more about your processes, you will also learn more about the Lean method itself and how best to apply it within your own organization.

### Lean Culture

"Culture eats strategy for breakfast."
— Attributed to Peter Drucker

Culture is an essential feature of an organization. It can elevate it to success or drive it to failure. It has a tremendous effect on employees' attitudes and behaviors, and yet many aspects of a culture are largely intangible and invisible. In common terms, an organization's culture is often thought of as "The way things are done" and "What we believe in."[5]

Some of the literature describes Lean culture in terms of readily observed management practices. For example, Mann describes Lean culture as a set of activities including leader standard work, visual controls, and accountability techniques (Mann 2010). I refer to this as the "surface culture" of Lean. Another common view of Lean culture is that it reflects an emphasis on "respect for people" (Liker 2004). This is the more personal and intangible part of the culture, which I refer to as Lean's "deep culture."

---

5    Culture has been described as a diverse set of features of an organization that include behavioral patterns, group norms, espoused values, formal philosophy, rules of the game, climate, embedded skills, habits of thinking, shared meanings, symbols, and formal rituals and celebrations (Schein 2010).

*Surface Culture*

The surface or visible part of a Lean culture provides a supportive platform for applying the Lean method. It is built upon the philosophy of bottom-up management, which is an increasingly popular approach that places greater emphasis and responsibility on the frontline workers. This type of management can be highly effective because it leverages the experience and intuition of *all* the employees and not just the experts. It is also the best way to get people to accept and even embrace change because it creates a feeling of "ownership" in how the work is performed. When it comes to sustaining an improved work process, involvement is good, but ownership is better!

Lean Principle #3: Bottom-Up Management

*Bottom-up participative management leads to a higher level of sustainable performance than top-down command and control management.*

As the associates improve their work and build their knowledge by applying the Lean method in a bottom-up fashion, the leaders provide a consistent and supportive environment through a series of "collaborative empowerment" practices. With these practices, the roles of "manager" and "worker" are quite different than in many traditional business environments.[6] Their relationship is not superior and subordinate, but rather coach and player, or even teacher and student.

As is typical of bottom-up management approaches, worker empowerment is an important practice. However, collaborative empow-

---

6    I will refer to these roles as "leader" and "associate." Leaders are individuals who have some level of supervision or oversight (e.g., team leaders, supervisors, managers, executives). Associates are other individuals who are directly responsible for carrying out the work processes. Of course, any one individual may be a leader in one context and an associate in another.

erment is not exactly the same as delegation, autonomous work groups, or self-managed teams. Rather than simply delegating responsibility to associates who make decisions independently, the leaders (and especially the frontline supervisors) work shoulder-to-shoulder with their associates, offering as much responsibility as the frontline associates are capable of handling. Both leaders and associates are jointly responsible for the quality of their work, even though the frontline supervisors remain accountable to upper level management.

---

Handling a Performance Problem at City Furniture
Andrew Koenig, Vice President

One of our supervisors came to me saying one of his associates was performing poorly. I asked the supervisor what he had done to help the associate succeed, and he responded: "There's nothing I can really do—this guy is just not cutting it. We have to let him go." I responded, "Well, it's your job to help him succeed, so I suppose we'll just have to get rid of both of you." The supervisor quickly agreed to see what he could do to help his associate.

---

A variety of Lean techniques are typically used to implement collaborative empowerment. These techniques are designed to work hand in hand with the Lean method, and they are associated with four essential management practices that form a logical cycle as shown on Figure 3. The collaborative empowerment practices include goal-setting, empowering, partnering, and coaching.

The practice of *goal-setting* involves the establishment of goals reflecting the organization's strategy. While it is important to obtain associate input, the leaders are ultimately responsible for setting and communicating clear expectations in the form of overall goals. Goal-setting provides critical guidance for associates who are empowered to drive the quality and performance of their processes. In essence, leaders set the goals regarding *what* needs to be done; then the associates take the lead in determining *how* to do the work in pursuit of those goals.

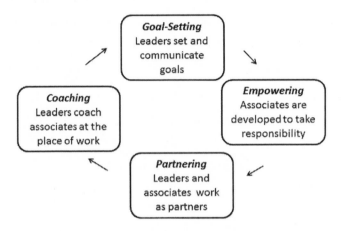

Figure 3. Practices of Collaborative Empowerment

Once goals are clearly established, associates can be *empowered* to take responsibility for the quality and improvement of their work. Empowering involves a general shift in focus from leaders to associates, requiring that associates are adequately trained and that they have access to necessary information, tools, resources, and support that provides them with the best possible opportunity to succeed.

*Partnering* involves a close, collaborative relationship between leaders and associates, as well as between different groups and departments within an organization. Information is openly shared between and among these various individuals and groups. Partnering techniques are centered on the formation of teams and their involvement in various types of meetings, events, and projects. The formation of properly structured teams is essential to facilitating the shift in emphasis from leaders to associates.

In the *coaching* practice, leaders apply Lean techniques that emphasize asking questions and providing guidance, rather than giving instructions and monitoring compliance. This includes helping associates develop knowledge and skills in the specifics of particular jobs and learning how to work as a team to apply the Lean method to the improvement of processes. Leaders must be available to spend time with associates and to coach them at the place where the work is performed, which is referred to as "the gemba." In a Lean system, leadership happens in the trenches.

As with the continuous learning practices of the Lean method, the specific tools and techniques used to implement these collaborative empowerment practices will vary greatly depending upon the organization's needs and resources.[7] For example, larger organizations may employ formally-structured policies and programs while smaller organizations may carry out these practices in a more informal way.

*Deep Culture*

While the surface culture involves practices at the organizational level, the deep culture of the Lean system operates at the deeper personal level of perceptions, attitudes, and behaviors. This deep culture is reflected in the simple philosophy that treating your employees well will lead them to treat you and your customers well. Organizations following this philosophy are marked by high levels of mutual trust and respect among their employees, customers, suppliers, and other stakeholders.

This leads to the fourth principle of Lean:

Lean Principle #4: Trust and Respect

*A culture built upon mutual trust and respect is more supportive of sustainable performance than a culture built upon fear and intimidation.*

---

7    Some of the commonly used Lean techniques and how they relate to each collaborative empowerment practice are presented in Chapter 8.

A deep culture of trust and respect represents the core of a Lean system. This core is necessary to facilitate the Lean method and the surface culture because associates must feel comfortable in sharing information and must be willing to take risks. This will not happen if they work in fear of punishment or retribution. How can a leader be an effective coach if he or she is not respected by associates? At the same time, how can associates be expected to accept empowerment from a leader whom they do not trust?

Trust and respect have powerful direct effects on human behavior that can have a significant positive impact on the organization.[8] Widespread respect leads to a condition of *engagement* where the associates are energized and fully committed to their jobs and to their organization. Pervasive trust tends to build an atmosphere of *transparency*, which is a high-confidence and low-fear environment that acts like a lubricant to take away friction in communication and leads to the development of positive working relationships.

The Lean method and the surface culture each contribute to an environment of trust and respect, especially when supported by programs and policies of recognition and celebration.[9] However, the most important factor in building and maintaining a strong, deep Lean culture is the type of personal character possessed and displayed by that organization's employees. Unfortunately, the personal character of associates and leaders is often the "elephant in the room" because it is so important, and yet, it is so infrequently discussed in an open and frank way.

In a Lean system, the personal characters of the associates and especially of the leaders must reflect four key values. These values are critical

---

8    Behavioral responses and organizational effects of trust and respect are explored in Chapter 9.
9    Refer to Chapter 11, Recognition and Celebration.

because they have the most direct effect on the level of mutual trust and respect. As shown on Figure 4, these "Lean values" include the norms of accountability and integrity, and the beliefs of respectfulness and trust-fulness.

|  | **Builds Respect** | **Builds Trust** |
|---|---|---|
| **Norms** | *Accountability*<br>• Take responsibility<br>• Keep commitments<br>• Deliver results | *Integrity*<br>• Be honest<br>• Be fair<br>• Show Loyalty |
| **Beliefs** | *Respectfulness*<br>• Be civil<br>• Be humble<br>• Sincerely care | *Trustfulness*<br>• Be willing to trust<br>• Have faith in others<br>• Be optimistic |

Figure 4. Lean Values

A person who holds himself or herself accountable will be respected by others; a respectful person will be perceived as showing respect. Likewise, a person with integrity will tend to be trusted; a person who exhibits trustfulness will be willing to extend trust to others.[10] People who believe in and follow these four values form the foundation for a culture of trust and respect.

### System Synergy

> "Synergy—the bonus that is achieved
> when things work together harmoniously."
>
> — Mark Twain

---

10   Examples of the four Lean values and associated behaviors are described in Chapter 10.

The Lean method and the Lean culture are both very effective in their own right. However, the full power of Lean results from the way in which the method and the culture are combined into a single system. When the method and culture are properly aligned, the method builds the culture while the culture strengthens the method.

The Lean method is a culture-building tool because mutual trust and respect is enhanced as associates build partnering relationships and see the positive effects of their waste-reduction efforts. The method also facilitates a respectful environment because it reduces the stress and conflict associated with the frustrating problems and obstacles that often arise in the course of daily work.

At the same time, a culture of trust and respect is necessary for the Lean method to be most effective. In a Lean culture, associates feel more engaged and are more motivated to sustain and search for process improvements as required by the Lean method. The transparency of a Lean culture also enhances the method because associates are more willing to take risks in suggesting improvements and are more likely to openly share their knowledge, experiences, and challenges.

The culture produces employees with focused energy and commitment while the method provides the technical means for structuring and guiding their efforts toward achieving organizational goals. The result is a group of highly engaged people who work together in a transparent environment for continual improvement of organizational performance. *This unique synergy of efficiency and humanity is the secret sauce of Lean.*

### What Lean is Not

Having described the essential Lean system in the previous sections, it is now helpful to clarify "what Lean is not." In the remainder of this chapter, Lean is compared and contrasted with ideas and programs that use the word "lean." This includes the phrase "lean and mean," Lean Six Sigma, and Lean Startup.

## Lean is not lean and mean

A common expression in business literature is that an organization needs to be "lean and mean." This implies cost-cutting and down-sizing. It is used to describe a type of belt-tightening or budget cutting in which resources are removed from an organization, often to the point where it hurts. The use of the word "lean" in this phrase is unfortunate because a Lean system is definitely not lean and mean.

While a Lean system does result in doing more with less, one key difference is that this is accomplished in a Lean system by removing wasteful activities that use resources in an unproductive way. A lean and mean budget-cutting approach implies that resources are simply reduced. Lean and mean also implies that quality may be compromised, or at least not improved as part of cutting costs. In a Lean system, improving quality is a natural result of applying the Lean method.

And, of course, a Lean system is definitely not "mean." Being mean implies an approach that is angry and certainly not very respectful or considerate of the needs of the employees. As should now be apparent to you, Lean is all about building a culture of respect and trust within an organization. Lean is about doing change *with* employees and not about doing change *to* employees.

## Lean is not Lean Six Sigma

An important step in addressing Lean's identity crisis is explaining the difference between a Lean system and a Lean Six Sigma program. The pervasive confusion over this difference may be a major obstacle to the advancement of Lean beyond manufacturing.

The Six Sigma program was originally developed at Motorola in the 1980s as a means for improving the reliability of complex electronic devices. The program was then popularized by Jack Welch in the 1990s when he adopted the program as the foundation for the corporate strategy of General Electric (Pande et al. 2000).

Six Sigma offers a broad range of tools and techniques for collecting, qualifying, and analyzing data. The program is built around highly skilled facilitators ("Black Belts"[11]) who have extensive training and experience in managing projects that involve the use of sophisticated statistical methods. Since its introduction in the 1980s, large manufacturing companies such as General Electric and Motorola have reported billions of dollars in cost savings from the application of Six Sigma.

While Lean and Six Sigma are similar in terms of their focus on improving the quality and productivity of work processes, they are actually quite different in a number of important ways. These differences are summarized in Table 1.

In terms of its overall approach, Six Sigma is data-driven. The method is built around general purpose tools that are mostly statistical and analytical in nature. The most common means for sustaining a Six Sigma improvement is statistical process control in which key metrics are tracked over time in relation to upper and lower control limits.

---

11   A "Black Belt" is a respected certification that requires extensive training and experience. The most prominent certification program is the CSSBB, or Certified Six Sigma Black Belt, which is offered by the American Society for Quality (2016).

Table 1. Six Sigma versus Lean

| | Six Sigma | Lean |
|---|---|---|
| General approach | Data-driven | People-driven |
| Method | Statistical and analytical | Visual and common sense |
| Sustaining mechanism | Statistical process control | Employee engagement and visual control |
| Improvement leaders | Specialists / Black Belts | Frontline employees |
| Improvement philosophy | "Let's study it properly" | "Just do it" |
| Required resources | Significant investment in training and structure | Significant commitment but can be scaled down |

This compares with Lean, which is a people-driven approach. While Lean certainly incorporates data and may include selected Six Sigma tools, the Lean method is more visual in nature and is generally designed to leverage common sense rather than analytical ability. Lean improvements are primarily sustained through the use of broadly accessible visual controls that guide the work of engaged associates.

Six Sigma improvements are identified within projects that may extend for many weeks or months. These projects are led by Black Belts who have in-depth knowledge of statistical concepts and techniques. Six Sigma follows the philosophy of "Let's study it properly" where the objective of the project is to optimize the process being analyzed. A Six Sigma project requires a substantial level of investment and each project is normally justified based on its expected monetary effects.

In contrast, Lean improvements are sometimes developed and implemented by frontline supervisors and associates during events that last from three to five days. At other times, improvements are made as part of the regular daily work routine. Lean requires significantly less training and is accessible to most employees, regardless of their educational background. The Lean philosophy is to be action-oriented in making small, incremental changes. While a Lean system does require a significant commitment of time and attention, the direct financial investment required is usually much less than Six Sigma.

Over the last ten years or so, we have seen an increased use of the term "Lean Six Sigma," which typically refers to programs that involve some combination of Lean tools and Six Sigma tools. While combining tools in this way can be useful,[12] the use of the term Lean Six Sigma contributes to the confusion surrounding Lean because it blurs the boundaries between Lean and Six Sigma. It is common to see Lean and Six Sigma lumped together in business literature and discussions.

The confusion that surrounds Lean and Six Sigma can lead to incorrect conclusions and misinformed decision-making. For example, leaders of many small and medium-size companies may see the large investment and sophisticated techniques associated with Six Sigma and, believing that Six Sigma and Lean are basically the same thing, may choose not to pursue either program. These individuals do not realize that Lean can be applied in a scaled-down fashion that is viable for even the smallest of organizations.

As another example, some concerns exist regarding the sustainability of improvements made in Six Sigma projects (Chakravorty 2010). Unfortunately, many articles in the business literature make no distinction between Lean and Six Sigma. Thus, readers may be left with

---

12  Further guidance on the use of Six Sigma within a Lean system is provided in Chapter 3, Plan of Action.

the mistaken impression that sustainability is a serious problem for both programs. In reality, sustainability is less of a problem in a Lean system because of the powerful effects of Lean culture on employee engagement and buy-in.

*Lean is not Lean Startup*

Over the past five years, "Lean Startup" programs have received a great deal of interest and attention (Ries 2011). Lean Startup is typically described as a means for starting a new business. It is essentially an approach to business planning and development involving rapid learning cycles, scientific experimentation, and continuous customer contact.

Lean Startup and the Lean method are different because they are used to improve different kinds of work activities. The Lean Startup method is applied to the *developmental work* that goes on within a start-up environment. In this highly uncertain environment, work activities are constantly changing as the business grows and progresses from an initial concept to a viable operation. This contrasts with the Lean method, which is applied to *stable work processes* that are repeatedly carried out within an established organization.

While Lean Startup and the Lean method involve different kinds of practices applied to different kinds of work, they do have similar features such as rapid learning cycles and customer focus, and it is possible to apply both approaches within the same organization. For example, Lean Startup results in the development and implementation of new work processes as the business grows and begins to operate. When these new processes are created and implemented, the Lean method can then be applied toward their ongoing improvement.

In addition to Lean Startup, other Lean-style approaches for design and development work can be used in conjunction with the Lean method. For example, "Agile" is a project management framework that has spawned popular software development methodologies such as "Scrum" (Sutherland 2014). In addition, "3P" is a development method that is often used by Lean organizations for designing products and Lean manufacturing processes (McDonnell & Locher 2013).

To illustrate the connection between the Lean method and an Agile project approach, consider a major information technology project that requires sophisticated information system design and development activities. While the frontline associates who will ultimately use this new system should have a great deal of involvement in the development project, it is unreasonable to expect them to actually drive system development activities because of the need for specialized expertise. For these types of projects, system development specialists typically lead the development effort using Scrum or some other type of Agile approach.

As the information system is implemented, it will often have a disruptive effect on the work processes of the system users. This will require major changes to the way in which they do their work, and it may even involve the creation of entirely new work processes. Implementing and training the associates on these new work processes is a part of the Scrum project. However, once the new processes are in place and reasonably stabilized, then the Lean method can be applied toward their future continuous improvement.

Even though the Lean method does not apply directly to developmental work, a Lean culture will certainly be a great asset in facilitating the radical changes that often result from such work. For example, IT projects can produce changes to the operation that are disruptive, painful, and subject to significant employee resistance. A strong Lean culture built upon mutual trust and respect will lead to associates who are more confident and trusting. As a result, they will be more willing to take on risks and to accept the uncertainty and disruption that comes along with these types of radical changes.

# Chapter 3

# Becoming Lean

"Progress is impossible without change,
and those who cannot change their minds cannot change anything."
— George Bernard Shaw

BUILDING A LEAN system is often described as a "journey." While application of the method will typically produce immediate results, extending these gains throughout the organization and building the right kind of culture takes a great deal of dedication. For those who are willing and able, this Lean journey produces unbeatable results and is well worth the effort.

## Leadership Commitment

Lean systems do not emerge spontaneously. While some isolated groups or departments may try to apply Lean within their own areas, implementing a Lean system throughout an entire enterprise *absolutely requires the full and persistent commitment of the top organizational leadership.* This includes an unwavering commitment to the personal values and character needed for a culture of trust and respect, as well as the new ways of thinking needed to fully implement the continuous learning method and the collaborative empowerment practices.

*Commitment to the Lean Values*

A culture of trust and respect depends upon having the "right people" in place—people who believe in and strive for the Lean values of accountability, integrity, respectfulness, and trustfulness. This, of course, begins with the top leaders who must set an example for the other leaders and for their associates. Leaders must hold themselves accountable to the highest personal standards of character, they must expect this accountability from others, and they must be vigilant in helping others maintain these standards.

A leader can practice Lean values in many ways.[13] For example, Lean improvements may reduce the number of hours required to complete a given task, leaving an associate without work. In this situation, *Lean cannot be used for the purpose of reducing head count*. Rather, leaders must be prepared to reassign associates to fill gaps in other areas, build up new business, and/or act as Lean facilitators in future kaizen events. A Lean transformation will only succeed if associates fully trust that their actions will not lead to layoffs.

*Commitment to New Ways of Thinking*

A Lean transformation almost always *requires a change in thinking*. Some of this new thinking centers on the Lean method and understanding the counterintuitive aspects of waste and flow. More broadly, the continuous learning approach of the Lean method requires a type of incremental or experimental thinking that is in contrast with the more common practice of immediately seeking out the optimal solution to any given problem (Rother 2010).

Individuals who have spent many years in a traditional command and control environment may find that some aspects of Lean are in

---

13   Further discussion of Lean values and the role of the leader is provided in Chapters 10 and 11.

conflict with their beliefs about the role of management and the relationship between manager and worker. For example, much of management involves an urgent need to produce short-term results. For top leaders, this is often reflected in pressure to meet aggressive monthly or quarterly goals. For frontline supervisors, this can translate to a need for committing all available resources to the completion of required work. Leaders and supervisors may feel they do not have time to conduct training, mentor associates, or even stop to fix a problem. A Lean leader must recognize that taking time to fix a problem or invest in associates *now* will end up saving a great deal of time *later on*, leading to *sustainable* results.

---

### Dealing with Recession at City Furniture
### Keith Koenig, CEO

We value our associates more than anything, and we had to let go of some of them during the last recession. We had sixty trucks a day going out instead of ninety, so there was just no need for so many delivery teams. We had four rounds of layoffs, resulting in the loss of about 300 jobs.

People are at the heart of our culture, but we had to prune the tree; otherwise, the tree was going to fall over and die. These were hard decisions, but all of those folks knew that they were not being laid off because of Lean.

Among all of those people, only one was upset. Each one got a generous severance package that hurt, and every one of them got a face-to-face conversation in which we told them "We're sorry." As I sat with each associate, the typical response was: "I get it. Boy, I sure like working here. Call me back when business gets better. I know what you guys are going through."

Many managers think of themselves as someone who tells others what to do—someone who directs and controls. While this is sometimes necessary even in a Lean system, a Lean culture emphasizes that managers should act more like mentors, coaches, or teachers, rather than like commanders. They should ask questions and listen rather than telling. In a sense, a manager must give up some level of control in order to get the best out of their associates. This also means managers must be more willing to share information than they may have been in the past.

These new ways of thinking can be quite difficult for managers, and even associates, to accept. Managers who have been burned in the past may be skeptical about extending trust and may feel they must maintain complete control to ensure work is done correctly and on time. At the same time, associates may not believe that their ideas and opinions actually matter, so they may find it difficult to make the transition from being told what to do to coming up with their own ideas. *A successful Lean transformation requires top leaders to commit to understanding, following, and encouraging these new ways of thinking throughout the organization.*

### Plan of Action

It is important to have an explicit plan of action. The plan should include specific activities, schedules, and assignments of responsibility unique to your organization. This book provides the essential concepts and outline for a Lean system, but each organization must develop its own "way" that connects with its own particular legacy, builds upon its special strengths, and addresses its most concerning weaknesses. It is likely that your plan will evolve over time, but you should always have a current plan to keep the implementation effort on track.

Should a Lean consultant be used? In larger companies, it is common to hire an experienced consulting firm that provides initial training and guidance until the organization can move forward on its own. In smaller companies, it may be possible to start without a consultant if key employees have sufficient training and experience, although this may be difficult because of day-to-day operational demands. As an alternative, it may be possible to obtain help from other Lean organizations in your local community. Lean organizations sometimes host tours and may be willing to offer support.

In creating a plan, it is important to understand the nature of the three components or building blocks of a Lean system and how they are related (see Figure 5). Each will be implemented in a very different way, but they are all essential. As you can see, the foundation consists of a deep culture of people who follow the Lean values. The surface culture of collaborative empowerment practices depends upon this deep foundation. Lastly, these two Lean culture components provide the underlying structure for building the continuous learning practices of the Lean method.

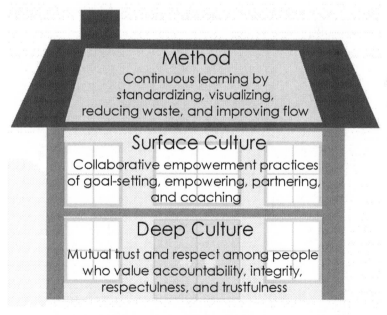

Figure 5. Essential Lean System Components

*Cultural Foundation*

To build your cultural foundation, start with an assessment of your current culture. This can be quite difficult because we are often unaware of the true nature of our culture and how it may differ from other cultures. Engagement and transparency are key indicators of the current culture's suitability.

Short of making a formal assessment, you can think about the extent to which employees are asked to participate in improving and sustaining work activities. Are workers viewed as primary drivers of quality, or do they simply follow directions? More broadly, are employees viewed as "active partners," "valuable assets," or merely one factor in the firm's success?

Many organizational leaders truly believe in and practice the value of respectfulness for the people around them. In developing a Lean system, these leaders should continue their cultural commitment and use the tools and practices of the Lean system to build and strengthen their culture. Other leaders may recognize the importance of trust and respect but may find it difficult or impractical to establish a trusting environment. For these leaders, the Lean method can be an invaluable tool for overcoming obstacles and building a strong foundation of trust and respect.

If trust and respect are limited in your existing culture, you should not pursue a Lean system unless top management is firmly committed to changing the culture. Also, be aware that early attempts to implement the Lean method in this type of environment can backfire, ultimately blocking systemic change.

Of course, any type of cultural change should be approached with great caution because it is almost always more difficult than it seems at the outset. Dealing with cultural change is a topic unto itself and outside the scope of this book. However, the first step is having the *desire* to change. Without that, change will not happen.

When assessing your culture, you should review your current organizational programs and policies to see what changes might be needed to support the new, Lean culture.[14] For example, policies and practices should be assessed to see which behaviors are being incentivized. Sales incentives creating end of the month pushes may encourage behavior counter to Lean thinking. In addition, leaders need to have the time to coach associates. This hands-on coaching may require a reduction in the size of the leader's span of control.

*Early Steps*

Early communication and training of associates is very important. Because of the associate-driven nature of the Lean system, it is imperative that associates feel connected with the transformation and, in fact, take some level of "ownership" in the effort. However, be sure to move quickly into hands-on experience. A "learning by doing" approach is the best way to understand the method.[15] Learning to recognize waste in your own work situation is a great way to get started and a very important early skill for associates to develop.

Initially, the Lean method should target "low hanging fruit." These are the areas in which a relatively small effort can produce quick and significant results. This approach helps build momentum and excitement among the associates. Some of these associates may become "Lean champions" who will be critical to continuing the transformation.

Once the Lean transformation is underway, further areas of improvement should be identified based on strategic need, perhaps through a hoshin planning activity.[16] This activity may involve examining the com-

---

14  Refer to Chapter 11 for further discussion of programs and policies.
15  You can use the Lean 7-Step method contained in Chapter 12 for your first attempt at Lean.
16  Refer to Chapter 8, Goal-Setting.

pany's core value streams that connect directly with external customers and then identifying particular areas of strategic importance.

*Later Steps*

As you begin to apply the method, you will realize the importance of having Lean suppliers. If you are fortunate enough to already have such suppliers, then seek out their help. If your suppliers are not Lean, then you will want to reach out to them at some point because Lean organizations typically have close working relationships with their suppliers. However, special challenges are associated with establishing a Lean supply chain, so this type of effort should not be an early priority.

It is generally best to focus initially on building up a Lean culture and implementing the Lean method before considering a Six Sigma approach.[17] While Six Sigma can certainly be applied within a Lean system, many of the techniques are quite sophisticated and difficult to learn, and, therefore, early emphasis on these techniques can become a significant obstacle to fully empowering your associates. This situation can send the wrong signal to employees regarding the importance of empowering them. By deferring the use of Six Sigma, Lean's focus on bottom-up management and mutual trust and respect can become well established as the dominant cultural environment. Later on, Six Sigma can be effectively applied within that type of environment.

## The Lean Journey

The Lean system offers a vision of how work should be performed and how people should be treated. The Lean method anticipates perfect work flowing without interruption. A Lean culture envisions leaders and associates who feel deep and lasting trust and respect for each other.

---

17    Refer to Chapter 2, What Lean Is Not.

But Lean is applied in the real world where people are certainly not perfect and our customers and suppliers may not understand or care about being Lean. Not everyone is trustworthy. An organizational culture is built around real human relationships, and everyone comes to the organization with a different set of habitual behaviors, attitudes, perceptions, and beliefs.

So, can the Lean vision of perfection ever be fully achieved? In reality, no it cannot. No Lean organization, not even Toyota, will ever say that it has reached perfection. This is not a problem because *the goal of a Lean system is not to achieve perfection, but rather to continually seek it!*

In a Lean system, we use the Lean principles as a means for correcting our biases and filling in our blind spots. The idea is to move toward a Lean vision, while at the same time recognizing that the vision can never be fully realized. Being Lean is not about reaching any particular plateau or meeting any particular standard. It is about being committed and participating in the journey.

For some individuals, this continual pursuit of perfection can become a transcendent purpose in its own right. Many Lean practitioners become almost like religious zealots in their passion for Lean. This passion can only help to engage employees further and may be especially useful in governmental or non-profit organizations where it is not possible to use the pursuit of profit as a motivating principle.

### Is Lean a Better Way?

> "The best way to predict the future is to create it."
> — Peter Drucker

Lean can take a great deal of time and commitment to build and sustain, and there are certainly other ways to run an organization. Traditionally, and to this day, many businesses have been quite profitable following a top-down philosophy, imposing strict authority, and maintaining tight control over employees. So is Lean actually better than using an authoritarian approach?

While sustaining Lean requires a substantial commitment, sustaining this old way of doing business also takes a great deal of effort. Fear and intimidation, rather than trust and respect, often become the dominant atmosphere in this type of business. This type of culture requires constant vigilance on the part of leaders. Employee responses when leaders are not watching can be unpredictable, sometimes involving counterproductive behaviors and even sabotage. An organization that relies on fear as its driving mechanism tends to be a pretty nasty and exhausting place to work, both for the managers and for the workers.

It is becoming more and more clear that this old way of thinking and managing will eventually become obsolete. The younger generation of workers is much less tolerant of disrespectful behavior directed toward them, and they are looking for positive environments in which to work. Leaders must meet many new expectations regarding sustainability and social responsibility. The Internet is bringing an unprecedented level of transparency to business, and attempts to conceal information are becoming futile. Power is shifting to the consumer, and poor responsiveness to the customer is more harmful than ever.

A Lean system provides the kind of respect that employees increasingly expect. Lean's focus on reducing waste is consistent with, and supportive of, the need for sustainability and social responsibility. Rather than fighting the trend toward increased transparency, Lean recognizes the value of openness and builds it into the system. The Lean method provides a systematic focus on the customer, and the culture of trust and respect naturally leads to responsiveness.

When recognizing the essence of Lean and how it relates to our rapidly changing society, it becomes clear that Lean really is a better way to run an organization—both for today and for the future. In fact, Lean may be the *only way* to ensure long-term success.

# PART TWO
# METHOD

# Chapter 4

# Visualizing a Process

"If you can't describe what you are doing as a process,
you don't know what you're doing."
— William Edwards Deming

THE LEAN METHOD begins with the concept of "process." In this chapter,
I explain what it means to view work as a process. I then proceed to
describe the two practices of standardizing a process and visualizing a
process. Process standardization is implemented through standard work
guides while the two key types of process visualization include visual
mapping and visual controls.

## Process View

The entire set of work activities in an organization can be quite com-
plicated. Taken as a whole, improving the work flow could seem like an
impossible task. However, if we break the overall work down into steps
or activities, it becomes more manageable. To that end, the purpose of
the process concept is to define a reasonable and meaningful "chunk" of
work to be assessed for improvement. Experience has shown that work
improvement is best understood one process at a time.

*A process is a stream of related activities that create value for process customers by transforming inputs into outputs.*

Engineers and software developers are trained to think about work as a process because that is a very effective way of devising and implementing improvements. However, if you are not trained in these fields, you may find it difficult to fully understand and internalize this important concept.

The concept of a process is essentially a perspective or "view"—it is merely a way of thinking about work. It is in the eye of the beholder. If you observe a work area, you will not literally *see* a process. Rather, you will see people working at desks, talking, and walking around. Process is merely a useful way of organizing our perception and thinking about these various observable work activities.

Examples of three types of work processes are depicted in Table 2. The inputs and outputs can be material, information, or human. Outputs are transformed version of the inputs, and the steps are the activities that transform the inputs into the outputs. In the table, the output of the biweekly payroll process is primarily information. The main output of the restaurant service process is a person who has finished his or her meal, and the output of the order fulfillment process is the receipt of material.

The series of activities we envision when thinking about a process are usually performed over and over again in the real world (perhaps by different people), and each execution of these activities may be (and is usually) somewhat different. So, a process is repetitive even though each execution of the process may be slightly different. A process in which each execution of the activities is radically different from the previous execution would be considered "unstable." It is normally necessary to achieve a reasonable level of stability in a process before Lean improvements can be made.

Table 2. Example Work Processes

| | Biweekly Payroll | Restaurant Service | Order Fulfillment |
|---|---|---|---|
| **Process Customer** | Employee being paid | Restaurant patron | Customer who places order |
| **Inputs** | Timesheet, pay rates | Restaurant patron, menu, raw ingredients | Customer order, stored goods |
| **Transforming Steps (Activities)** | Capture hours worked, calculate payment amount, prepare paycheck | Greet customer, take order, prepare meal, serve meal, customer pays bill | Order placed, acknowledgment sent, goods packed, goods shipped, order received |
| **Outputs** | Paycheck disbursement, accounting record | Completed meal, check paid | Goods received |

Processes often run across departmental boundaries and, therefore, tend to be cross-functional. This is important because people often have a "silo view" of work, focusing on what happens within their own department or functional area. As a result, many problems and inefficiencies are typically found in the "hand-offs" between departments, and it is common for one department's operations to be optimized at the expense of another.

Defining cross-functional processes and incorporating all relevant departments will normally help to reveal these problems and set the stage for solutions. Cross-functional processes are usually more challenging to improve, but their improvement often leads to bigger payoffs.

### Standard Work

> "There can be no improvement where there are no standards."
>
> — Masaaki Imai, Author of *Kaizen* (1986)

Lean literature refers to the technique of "standard work" as a means for documenting work activities and procedures. In a process, this documentation is used to ensure the work is conducted in the best possible way by all individuals. It is also used to train new associates and current associates who need to learn an improved version of the process.

The standardization of work plays a critical role in learning because it captures and communicates the current "best way" of performing that work. It is the basis for initial learning (training) and then continual learning (discovery) of the nuances of the work and its improvement. You must first document standard work before moving forward to make improvements.

You might think of standard work as a kind of standard operating procedure. Standard work *is* like a standard operating procedure in presenting a *fixed* and uniform definition of how the work should be performed. However, standard work is unlike a standard operating procedure in that it must be *flexible*. Standard work provides structure because leaders establish the procedures and provide the authority for making changes to the standard practice. Associates are empowered to learn and improve while leaders still maintain organizational control. Standard work balances learning with production.

Standard work is especially important in Lean systems because work that flows tends to be highly synchronized. This means that each actor in the process works very closely with other actors. There is little or no "buffer" between them. In this situation, it is critical for each associate to understand his or her own work and how that work relates to the rest of the process. This kind of awareness is enabled by standard work.

As individuals learn more and more about the process, the accumulation of this knowledge is captured in the *standard work guide*. A standard work guide is intended to be a "living document" that can be updated frequently to reflect further improvements that are identified as part of the continuous learning cycle. In this sense, standard work is a kind of challenge to process associates. It defines the current way of doing things so that associates have a baseline upon which they can improve.

The standard work guide can take many forms such as a checklist, an instruction sheet, a timeline chart, or a physical layout chart (see Figures 6 and 7).[18] The standard work guide should be easily understandable to the process actors conducting the work. In addition, it should not be tucked away in a drawer, but rather, it should be easily accessible and visible so that it can be frequently checked by the associates. More recently, standard work has been documented in the form of short videos, which can be very effective.

### ED Admitted Patient, Information Flow Time Line

Date Prepared | Manual Tracker Time `< - - >` | Facilitation Time `/X/X/X` | Wait Time `< >` | Target 73 min

| Responsible Party | Steps | Work | Tracker Notice | Wait | Work Time ( In Minutes) |
|---|---|---|---|---|---|
| MD | Complete Blue Sheet | 5 | | | |
| | Hit PMD on Tracker | 1 | 67 | | `<- - - - - - - Trigger Heads-Up - - - - - - - - ->` |
| | Speak with PMD | 5 | | | |
| | Cisco Transfer to RN | 1 | | | |
| | Admitting MD enters CPOE | 10 | | | |
| RN | Receive and Chart Orders | 5 | | | |
| | Complete SBAR | 7 | | | |
| | Facilitate Flow | | 67 | | Respond to PMD Trigger on Tracker, Facilitate Flow |
| | Chart on Transporter Rack | 1 | | | |
| | Fax SBAR to Floor | 2 | | | |
| Unit Secretary | Blue Form in, Call PMD | 1 | | < 30 | `<Try for 30 minutes>` |
| | Cisco Transfer to ED Doc | 1 | | | |
| | Log Call on Tracker | 2 | | | |
| | Bed Request | 5 | 67 | | `<- - - Trigger Heads-Up - - - ->` |
| | Schedule w/Transporter | 1 | 15 | 15 | `<15 min notice>` |
| | Proactively find Bed | | | 15 | |
| | Total | 47 | | 60 | 73 min |

Figure 6. Standard Work Guide (Timeline Chart)
Courtesy: Sheridan Healthcare, Amichay Porges

---

18 The Training Within Industry Job Instruction Sheet may be useful as a standard work guide. Refer to Chapter 8, Empowering.

---

### XSolutions Support Ticket Handling Process
### Standard Work Guide for Techs

1) Client requests support

2) Open ticket and send acknowledgment to client
*Goal: within 10 minutes from client's support request*
      -> Use email template "Support Ticket Acknowledgment Email"

3) Triage the ticket and make escalation decision
      -> Follow "Support Ticket Escalation Rules"

4) Work the ticket
      -> Use Ticket Support system

5) Fix the issue and call or email the client to confirm the fix
*Goal: within 45 minutes of opening the ticket*

6) Document the ticket
      -> Use Ticket Documentation screen
*Goal: document all tickets by the end of the day*

---

Figure 7. Standard Work Guide (Checklist)

## Visual Mapping

Two types of visual mapping are described in this section. The most common and iconic form of mapping is the value stream map. Also described is the spaghetti chart, which can be very useful if excessive walking and/or transportation is observed.

*Value Stream Map*

A value stream map is a tool that helps to depict process activities and their interactions.[19] Each associate who works on a particular process will have a particular mental image of how the process actually works. The value stream map provides a means for recording these images on a physical map. There are various possible styles of value stream maps. The traditional style, which often describes an enterprise-wide "macro view," is illustrated in Figure 8. An alternative flowchart style, which is more useful for a "micro view," is shown in Figure 9.

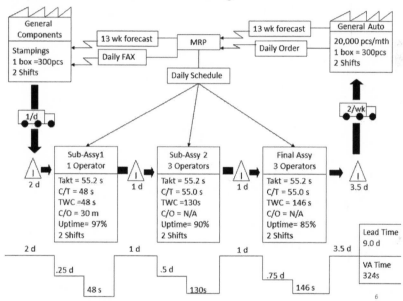

Figure 8. Value Stream Map (Macro View)
Courtesy: Transformation Management, LLC

A value stream map has a direction or time sequence representing the flow of activities, leading from input to output. Although most processes involve some flow of information, each process will involve a

---

19   Lean literature refers to the concept of "value stream." Although a value stream is often viewed at an enterprise level as a set of processes (Rother and Shook 1999), I will use the terms "value stream" and "process" interchangeably.

primary flow of material (e.g., assembling a product), information (e.g., processing an insurance claim) or people (e.g., treating a patient or educating a student).

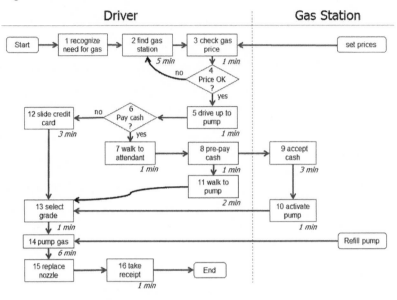

Figure 9. Value Stream Map (Micro View)

A value stream map provides a common language and a single reference point for team members to think and talk about the process to be improved. This is important because different process actors will often have different opinions about how the process actually works, and mapping out the process will bring these differences to the surface where they can be reconciled. You must map out a process in order to understand it fully. A value stream map makes problems visible. Only after problems are visible can they be addressed.

*Spaghetti Chart*

Another useful tool in understanding and visualizing a process is a spaghetti chart. This type of chart is a diagram of a physical work space with lines representing the typical walking paths of process associates. In a wasteful environment, these lines often look like cooked spaghetti.

In the example shown in Figure 10 (Duncan and Ritter 2014), the excessive level of walking is illustrated by the many walking paths displayed on the "Before" section of the chart. The positive effects of the improvements on process flow and the waste of walking are clearly shown by the fewer and more direct paths that appear on the "After" section of the chart.

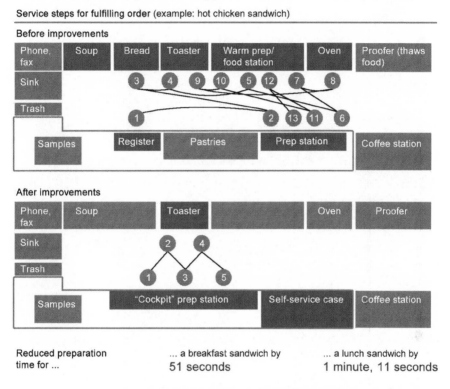

Figure 10. Before and After Spaghetti Chart

## Visual Controls

Various types of visual tools are used to guide and control the execution of a process. Some tools, such as red flags and green flags, indicator lights, clocks, or other status devices, indicate the real-time status of the process. Other tools, display monitors, charts, and/or white boards, provide feedback on the prior performance of the process.

With visual control, there is less need for leaders to provide feedback regarding job performance. Properly designed visual controls can provide a great deal of information in a highly intuitive way. Examples of visual controls are shown in Figure 11. In the figure, the current status of the process is represented by a red flag. Hourly performance is shown on the computer monitor. Other visual controls are provided by signage and floor markings.

Visual controls will often incorporate certain process metrics used to track the improvement progress and its effect on process performance. These metrics reflect the most important anticipated performance gains and are used to gauge the status and progress of implementation efforts. Examples of process metrics that might be important to a customer include "percentage of phone calls answered within three rings," or "percent of furniture deliveries made at the promised time."

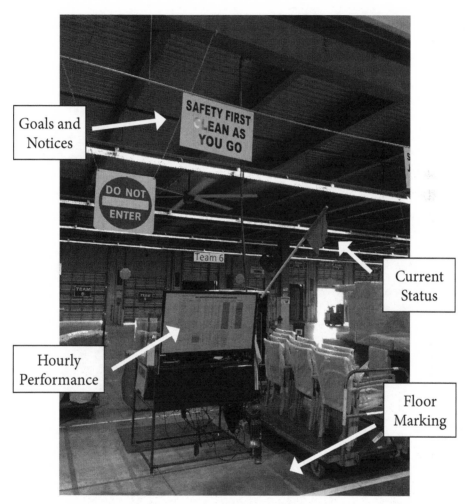

Figure 11. Visual Control Examples
Courtesy: City Furniture

# Chapter 5

# Value and Performance

"There is only one boss. The customer.
And he can fire everybody in the company from the chairman on
down, simply by spending his money somewhere else."
— Sam Walton

B ECAUSE WASTE IS defined as anything that does not produce value for customers, it is important to understand who these customers are and what they actually value. In this chapter, I define "process stakeholders" to include customers and other individuals who have an interest in the process. I then describe the kinds of value that these stakeholders are looking for and I show how these value factors are used in assessing the current level of process performance.

### Process Stakeholders

Process stakeholders are individuals who benefit from, or who otherwise care about, the performance of the process. These individuals are important because they define expectations about the types of value that should be generated by the process.

When improving a process, much attention is given to "process customers" because they are the individuals who use the output generated by the process. In effect, the process exists to satisfy their needs. Therefore, the effectiveness of the process is directly tied to their satisfaction.

For some processes, process customers are the external customers. For example, the process customer for a meal service is the restaurant patron. For other processes, the process customer is an *internal* customer. For example, the process customers of a payroll process are the employees who receive and use the payments generated by that process. If processes are properly aligned with organizational goals, then high-performing processes that satisfy internal customer needs will ultimately lead to the fulfillment of external customer needs.

In addition to process customers, the other key process stakeholder is the organization itself. I will refer to individuals who represent the organization as "organizational agents." These individuals include owners, directors, executives, managers, and other individuals who have some level of oversight responsibility and who represent the interests of the organization as a whole.

### Stakeholder Value

Process stakeholders define what they expect from the process in terms of "value factors." In effect, these statements of value define the ideal process.[20] Defining these value factors is an important consideration because it is common to assume that we know what customers want when, in fact, we really don't. In addition, the wants and needs of stakeholders will sometimes change over time, so it is important to continually think about process stakeholders and what they value.

The four types of value defined in the Lean method are: quality, speed, productivity, and compliance. Quality can be thought of as fea-

---

20   Refer to Chapter 7, Lean Vision.

tures of the process output; speed is the time required to produce the process output; productivity is the level of output that can be produced with a given level of resource; compliance involves the extent to which formal or informal standards and policies established by the organization are complied with.

*Quality* can take on many different meanings depending upon the process and the customer. For example, quality in a payroll process may depend on making correct payments. In a restaurant service process, quality is based on meeting the customer's expectation for food taste. In an order fulfillment process, quality may depend on the customer receiving a complete and accurate order.

*Speed* involves the time between specific events. In this case, there are usually particular intervals that are most important to process customers. For example, restaurant patrons are sensitive to the time it takes to prepare and deliver a meal. In an order fulfillment process, the lead time from placing an order to receiving it is usually the most important interval.

*Productivity* considers the resources required to produce the process outputs. Specifically, productivity is the level of output that can be produced with a given level of resource. In identifying value factors for productivity, organizational agents identify what they believe are the critical resources and costs for the target process.

*Compliance* relates to the organization's standards and policies. Many of these are established to protect process actors,[21] such as standards for work safety and limits on the level of physical and mental stress associated with the work. These standards may be set internally, or they may be dictated by external organizations, such as the safety standards established by OSHA. Other standards are established to protect external customers, such as FDA regulations.

---

21 "Process actors" are the individuals who actually carry out the process.

## *Process Performance*

> "Data is of course important...
> but I place the greatest emphasis on facts."
> — Taiichi Ohno, Toyota

Improving a process means that greater value is delivered to process stakeholders. Using the value factors identified by process stakeholders as a baseline, the current performance of a process can then be assessed in terms of the actual value created. A high performance process is one in which a high level of value is produced for the stakeholders. If value production is not as high as it could be, then that defines a "problem."

In the Lean method, problems are gems. They provide opportunities for improvement. Finding a problem helps you to understand what doesn't work. Overcoming obstacles and solving a problem helps you to understand what does work. This is all part of the continuous learning cycle. The immediate problem is solved, and you are now more knowledgeable in addressing future problems that may arise as things change, new people come in, or new demands are placed on the process.

The assessment of process performance is based on facts gathered through the observations and perceptions of process stakeholders. However, these facts should be validated and supported by process metrics whenever possible. Stakeholder perceptions can be misinformed and/or biased, and the use of metrics will increase the likelihood of obtaining an objective and unbiased view.

A valid process metric should be directly driven by the performance of the target process and *not by other activities that are outside the scope of the target process*. For example, sales and gross profits are not typically useful process metrics because they are affected by so many processes within an organization. An example of a valid process metric for serving a customer in a quick service restaurant might be average wait time. This is a good metric for that process because it is driven primarily by activities within the scope of the process.

Metrics for quality performance vary depending upon the nature of the process and how process customers define quality. Examples of quality metrics shown in Table 3 include percent defects, customer satisfaction ratings, and other measurements that characterize process outputs.

Table 3. Value Factors and Process Metrics

| Value Type | Value Factor | Example Process Metrics |
|---|---|---|
| Quality | Features of the process output | • Customer satisfaction rating<br>• Defect rate |
| Speed | Time required to produce output | • Total cycle time<br>• Lead time<br>• Value-added time percentage |
| Productivity | Level of output produced per unit of resource | • Person-hours per customer served<br>• Average inventory level<br>• Distance traveled per unit produced |
| Compliance | Meeting organizational standards and polices | • Standard achieved (yes/no)<br>• Days since last accident |

A primary metric for speed performance is the total cycle time for the target process. While various definitions of cycle time exist, I will use the term to represent the normal total time from the beginning to the end of the target process, based on a typical batch size and including typical waiting or delays. For example, if a batch of fifty invoices is normally paid in an accounts payable process, then the process cycle time would be the period from when the process begins until the fifty invoices are paid.

Metrics for productivity performance might incorporate person-hours, operating expense dollars, head count, or other measurements of resource usage or consumption. These are combined with measurements of output, such as number of service transactions or number of products produced. For example, one productivity metric might be the number of person-hours required per customer served.

Compliance metrics may be simple "yes/no" indications of whether or not the process actually complies with the appropriate standard. For example, a process will either comply or not comply with a particular financial regulatory standard. However, some compliance metrics involve other types of measurements, such as the number of days that have passed since the last safety incident.

While data should be used to the greatest extent possible, it is important to recognize the limitations of data. Developing accurate and reliable metrics can be difficult, and many areas of the business world simply cannot be captured in quantitative measures. It is important not to become overly focused on measurements and lose sight of the value of direct observation and common sense.

---

How Much of Business Is Measurable?

I use this thought experiment in my classes:

"A CEO is locked in a room and has no contact with the outside world other than the data streams fed into computer monitors. How much of the information the CEO needs to run the company is available on those monitors?"

Students come up with various answers, but they are typically in the range of 10 to 20 percent or less.

# Chapter 6

# Waste and Root Cause

"If I had an hour to solve a problem, I'd spend 55 minutes
thinking about the problem and 5 minutes
thinking about solutions."

— Albert Einstein


W ASTE IS A fundamental concept in the Lean method because it is
the way in which we define the problem. In this chapter, I describe the seven classic types of waste and I explain the concept of "root
cause" and why it is important in identifying potential Lean solutions.

## Waste as the Problem

The first principle of Lean involves the Lean concept of waste:[22]

Lean Principle #1: Waste

*Work processes are most effectively improved by eliminat-
ing waste. Waste is the problem.*

*Waste is any activity in a process that does not produce value for pro-
cess stakeholders.*

---

22   In Lean literature, waste is often referred to as "muda."

Waste is one of the most powerful and useful concepts of the Lean method. All improvement activities revolve around identifying and eliminating waste. The focus on waste ensures that maximum value is delivered to the customer and that customer needs and wants are continually assessed in a systematic way. This continual learning and improvement acts to increase the quality and responsiveness of the products or services offered by the organization.

At the same time, this focus on reducing waste improves productivity because wasteful activities are minimized or eliminated, thus allowing resources to be applied directly to the satisfaction of customers. This focus attacks bureaucratic aspects of the organization, which naturally leads to a reduction in cost.

### Types of Waste

Because waste involves activities that do not produce value, finding waste requires examination and thought about *activities* in the current process. However, *recognizing* waste within these activities can be a challenge. This recognition is deceptively difficult because waste is often hidden within our "normal" ways of doing things. We become accustomed to these ways, and we then accept wasteful activities as normal. Before you can recognize waste, it is important to understand the different kinds of waste. The seven classic types of waste are summarized on Table 4.[23]

### Defects

The first type of waste is "defects." In essence, defects occur when something has gone wrong. A defective output is one that fails to meet the needs of the process customers. A defective activity involves any type of

---

23  Lean literature sometimes refers to an eighth waste that involves the waste of human capability. This is a different type of waste than the other seven, and it is more appropriately covered in Part Three: Culture.

error or mistake that causes material or information to be reprocessed or a service to be redelivered. This type of waste is probably the easiest to understand because it relates to our conventional concept of waste or trash.

Table 4. Seven Classic Types of Waste

| Waste Type | Description |
|---|---|
| Defects | Errors, mistakes, or inadequate outputs that cause the work to be redone |
| Waiting | People waiting for material or information, or material or information waiting to be processed |
| Excessive Production | Creating too much material or information |
| Excessive Inventory | Holding more material or information than is needed to satisfy customer demand |
| Excessive Walking | Unnecessary walking or other motions of people to produce the desired output |
| Excessive Processing | Performing more work than is necessary to produce the desired output |
| Excessive Transportation | Unnecessary movement of material or transmission of information to produce the desired output |

Some common examples of defect waste are missing, incomplete, or inaccurate information on paper forms or data screens. In a restaurant service process, a defect might be an incorrect order or a meal that does not meet the customer's taste expectations.

*Waiting*

The second type of waste is waiting. This waste can include people or machines that remain idle because they are waiting for inputs or the completion of a prior activity. They may be waiting for someone else or for the arrival of material or information. However, the waste of waiting is also relevant from the perspective of the material or information itself.

For example, an in-box full of unread emails represents information that is waiting for something to happen to it.

Waiting can be relatively easy to recognize, although we may not see it as waste. Customers wait for a response from an organization or an organization waits for a response from a customer. Customers wait at a service counter; they wait on the phone.

Reducing the waste of waiting will improve the speed performance of the process. Of course, this assumes that reduced waiting is accomplished in a productive manner, for example, by eliminating an unnecessary step, and not simply by rushing beyond a reasonable pace that can lead to other types of problems.

### Excessive Production and Inventory

The third and fourth types of waste are related. These are excessive production and excessive inventory. In manufacturing and logistical processes, these relate to the production and storage of material. In service processes, they relate to the production and storage of information. In general, these two wastes involve producing material or information at a rate that is greater than the pace required to satisfy customer demand.[24] This situation can be described as "*overproduction.*"

Excessive production is the creation of more material or information than is currently needed to serve the customer. For example, preparing a voluminous report with a great deal of irrelevant information is an overproduction waste. Excessive production naturally leads to excessive inventory, which is holding more material or information than is currently needed. Of course, in these cases, it is necessary to define the level of production or inventory that "is currently needed," which is a matter of judgment.

---

24  In Lean literature, the pace of production required by customer demand is often described using the term "takt time," which is the "correct" amount of time required to produce or supply one unit of product.

*Excessive Walking, Processing, and Transportation*

The fifth, sixth, and seventh types of waste are also related. These include excessive walking, processing, and transportation. These are *non-productive activities* in the sense that they are not needed to produce value for the customer. These relate to what is commonly thought of as "inefficiencies."

Excessive walking involves any walking, hand movements, or other motions that are not necessary to produce the required process outputs. Excessive processing includes any unnecessary steps or lengthy activities that require more time or effort than is necessary to produce the desired outputs. Excessive transportation involves moving material or information more than is necessary.

These types of waste may be more difficult to recognize and, as with excessive production and excessive inventory, they involve subjective judgments. Bureaucratic organizations are filled with non-productive activities, such as requiring too many approvals and having too many touch points.

The Lean concept of waste is sometimes difficult to accept because it is counter to many of the conventional ways in which we think about work and business performance. An example of conventional thinking is the idea that we should double-check our work or that quality control inspectors are useful and important. In Lean thinking, quality control is viewed as excessive processing, a type of waste that could be eliminated if the work were performed correctly the first time.

Other examples relate to inventory and purchasing materials. We normally view inventory as an asset, we transport full truckloads of materials in order to minimize the unit shipping cost, and we order large quantities of materials in order to obtain volume discounts and minimize the unit purchasing cost. These actions result in waste if more goods are obtained, held, or transported than are actually needed.

Lean does not mean that all of the above ideas are totally incorrect. It just means that we tend to be biased toward accepting these ideas as a normal part of doing business. The Lean principle of waste challenges us to view these activities as something that might be changed in order to improve the associated process.

### Root Causes of Waste

Waste is the result of a number of different causes or factors, some of which are under the control of the organization and some of which are not. A controllable cause behind a problem is referred to as a "root cause." Because identifying the root cause of a problem will reduce or eliminate the problem, identifying the root cause of the waste problem will naturally lead to a possible solution.

It is important to distinguish between root causes and symptoms and not merely to treat the symptom. For example, a headache is a common symptom, but there are many possible causes for that headache. Finding and treating the actual root cause is necessary if the headache is to be relieved permanently.

In some cases, the root cause may be relatively simple. For example, the root cause of an over-stuffed email in-box may be the work habits of the in-box owner. The root cause of excessive walking may be the physical layout of the office space. In other cases, the root cause may be more complex. For example, the root cause behind defects and delays may be found in procedure design, training methods, and/or many other areas.

Identifying a root cause can be difficult. Because there are usually multiple factors that lead to waste, it may not be clear which factor is the most important in producing the waste. In addition, the various factors may interact with each other in influencing the observed waste. Root causes are often not immediately obvious and may require some detective work to reveal.

Finding every single root cause for the observed waste is not practical, nor is it necessary in the Lean method. In Lean, identifying one meaningful root cause may be sufficient in defining a useful improvement. Remember, in Lean we will continue to search for other root causes and associated improvements as part of the never-ending learning and improvement cycle.

# Chapter 7

# Process Flow

"Swift even flow works; it worked in times past, it works today,
and it can be expected to work in the future."

— Roger W. Schmenner, Professor Emeritus of Operations
Management (2004)

IMPROVING FLOW INVOLVES the development and implementation of improvement actions designed to reduce or eliminate waste. Removing waste improves flow, leading to an increase in value production for stakeholders. In this chapter, I explain the concepts of "flow" and "Lean vision," and I describe the Lean improvement cycle and the various types of solutions that are commonly deployed in this cycle.

## *Flow as the Solution*

The second Lean principle states that the means for eliminating waste is to improve flow. The principle is stated as follows:

Lean Principle #2: Flow

*Flow is the vision of an ideal work process. Improving flow reduces waste.*

*Flow is a pattern of work in which the process activities are performed in a constant and uninterrupted manner.*

The essential feature of work that flows is the lack of interruptions experienced in the timing and sequence of process activities. It may be useful to think of a process as a kind of river. If the river flows straight and at a constant rate throughout, then you have effective flow. If the river has bends or rapids that cause turbulence, or if the water pools up behind a dam, then you have interruptions in the constant flow pattern.

The concept of flow provides guidance to those who wish to improve work by eliminating waste. Flow is what ideal work should look like. It is the means by which waste can be eliminated. It is the basis for the Lean vision that is created as a goal to be sought. In a process that flows, every activity produces value. There is no waiting or interruption in the sequence of activities. As further described below, flow is characterized by small batches of work and just-in-time synchronization.

## Batch Size

Flow is an abstract concept that can be difficult to understand and/or accept because it may be contrary to conventional thinking about the nature of efficient work. People seem to be generally biased toward a "batch and queue" pattern, where large batches are thought to be optimal. Batch and queue involves working on large "batches" of work units,[25] and then placing the completed units into a queue or waiting line. The queue may take the form of a pile of papers, physical inventory, or a backlog of service work to be performed in a subsequent step.

It is common to conduct work in large batches and to buy and/or ship large batches of material in order to achieve a low unit cost. The Lean method recognizes the hidden costs and other disadvan-

---

25   In production or logistical processes, a work unit is typically a single item of the product being produced or shipped. In service processes, a work unit may consist of a single served customer or a single transaction.

tages associated with this "batch and queue" approach. In the Lean method, the ideal flow condition occurs when only one unit of work is completed at a time. Even though this is an ideal vision that may never be reached, this way of thinking is difficult to understand for many people.

For example, we generally believe that it is best to set up a particular work activity and then repeat that activity for many work units at once (in a large batch) so that frequent work set-ups can be avoided. We also recognize that performing the same activity over and over again on multiple work units may improve our speed and lead to greater efficiency as we become accustomed to the activity.

While larger batch sizes will, in fact, reduce the number of set-ups and may reduce the time required per unit, Lean thinking recognizes that reducing the batch size will be beneficial in many other, more important ways. For example, *large batches hide defects*. Smaller batches allow quick detection of defects so the problem can be fixed before more defects are created. Smaller batches also reduce the level of *inventory* and the *lead times* necessary for a unit of work to travel through the process.

Batches and the related queues represent interruptions in the constant flow of a process; therefore, flow can be improved by reducing batch size. Although it is not always practical, the theoretically perfect form of flow is "one-piece flow" in which the batch size is "one."

As an example, the batch involved in an accounts payable process could be represented by the number of invoices typically processed at one time. If 100 invoices need to be paid per month, executing the process once per month would result in a batch of 100 invoices to be paid at one time. If the process is executed twice per month, then the average batch size would be 50 invoices.

The change in paying invoices from once a month to twice a month represents an improvement in the flow of the process because the batch size is reduced from 100 invoices to 50 invoices. The extreme case here would be to literally process one invoice at a time, in which case the batch size would be "one" and one-piece flow would be achieved. While this may not be a practical solution, Lean thinking leads us to consider reducing the batch size in order to improve flow.

*Pull*

Lean literature refers to the concept of "pull" or "just in time." Pull is a work practice in which goods are not produced and/or services are not provided until the process customer is ready for the goods or services. No one produces a good or service or processes material or information until someone downstream has requested it. This practice is normally applied to production scheduling or the delivery of materials in a supply chain, although it can also apply to service processes.

In service processes, pull means that service begins exactly when the customer is ready. In manufacturing and logistical processes, it means that goods are produced or delivered just when they are needed. If activities are conducted too early, then goods or information must "wait" in inventory. If produced too late, then the customer must wait. If produced just in time, the waiting is eliminated.

Pull can help to improve flow. Only creating a product or service when it is needed by a customer will naturally eliminate waste such as waiting, excessive production, and excessive inventory. Pull systems are agile and responsive to customer demand so there is less need for accurate forecasting.

The opposite of pull is push. Push occurs when goods or services are provided before a customer really needs them. For example, sales reps often use a push practice in which customers are sold large volumes of goods that exceed the customer's needs in the short term. This might be justified based on a volume discount or special promotional price. These push-type techniques produce waste and are not consistent with Lean thinking.

As an example of how a process can be improved by moving from push to pull, we can consider the state of the printing industry (Womack and Jones 2003). Previously, the printing industry involved carefully making forecasts of the number of books that might be purchased over an extended period of time and then printing and distributing large batches, or runs, of these books. The books were then pushed out into the distribution channels, leading to excessive inventory and the need for additional transportation to return unsold books to the publisher.

With the emergence of more advanced technology, it is now possible to print one book at a time, in effect, a batch size of one and still be cost-effective. Now, it is common for a book to be "printed on demand" only after an order for that book has been received. By moving to this pull practice, the waste of excessive inventory and transportation has been greatly reduced. With eBook technology, there is a further reduction in waste because of the shift from material transportation to information transportation (downloading an eBook).

### Lean Vision

A Lean vision is an image of how the current process might look if it had no waste and exhibited perfect flow conditions. This image might be a mental image that is formulated and discussed among key process stakeholders. However, the Lean vision may also be documented in the form of a "future value stream map." This map is usually prepared at an abstract or conceptual level to represent the vision. Exact details for designing this process are usually not known at the time the vision is created.

The Lean vision's purpose is to provide associates with direction and challenge as they learn how to move toward the vision by making small improvements to the process. For example, the Lean vision for a process might include one-piece flow and production of goods or services that are triggered by demand in a just-in-time fashion. The vision could also include a flow pace that exactly matches the pace of demand without any buffers. In a sense, the Lean vision is a synthesis of the value factors held by the process stakeholders, but expressed using the Lean concept of flow.[26]

It is important to recognize that the Lean vision is not the same as quantitative goals, which are often set at the beginning of or during a kaizen event ("event goals"). These goals are typically represented by particular metrics and may provide a connection with broader organizational goals ("Key Performance Indicators" or KPIs) and with a strategic plan. The Lean vision is not meant to replace these quantitative goals. Rather, it is developed so that employees can align their process improvement efforts in a direction that is consistent with the organization's mission and strategy.

## Improvement Cycle

Improving the flow of a process is essentially an iterative design activity in which possible improvements are first identified and evaluated and then one or more improvements are selected and implemented. In Lean and other process improvement literature, this cycle is often referred to as PDCA, where the letters stand for Plan, Do, Check, and Act. This is essentially a form of scientific thinking that has also been described as a "kata" by Rother (2010). In a Lean system event, this improvement cycle has many inputs, as depicted in Figure 12.

---

26   Refer to Chapter 5, Stakeholder Value.

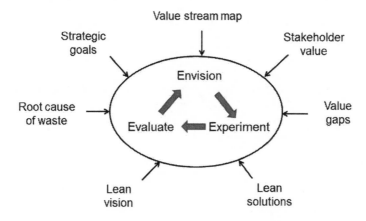

Figure 12. Lean Improvement Cycle

In practical terms, the Lean improvement cycle results in the implementation of certain changes or actions that lead to the improvement of a process. These actions can be thought of as "solutions" that act to solve the problem of waste by improving process flow.[27] The effect of any one solution may be small or large, but it is the accumulated effect of these actions that leads to long-term and sustainable process improvement.

As seen in Table 5, there are various types of improvement actions, including changes to work assignments, layout and facility design, procedures and methods, activity sequence, and tools, equipment, and information technology. Some solutions are commonly associated with Lean systems while others are more general in nature. Commonly used Lean solutions are noted in Table 5 and are described in the remainder of this section.

## Work Assignments

Work assignment solutions include changes in who conducts which activities. One of the key problems to be addressed in this area is over-

---

27 In Lean literature, these solutions are often referred to as "countermeasures" because they are intended to counteract the negative impact of waste.

loading an individual, who can then become a bottleneck and impede the flow of work. Avoiding a bottleneck will reduce waiting waste and may have other positive effects.

Table 5. Common Lean Solutions

| Type of Improvement | Lean Solutions |
|---|---|
| 1) Work Assignments | • Workload balancing |
| 2) Layout / Facility Design | • 5S technique<br>• Work cells |
| 3) Procedures / Methods | • Batch size reduction<br>• Kitting |
| 4) Activity Sequence | • Reorder activities<br>• Sequential to parallel |
| 5) Tools / Equipment / IT | • Kanban<br>• Poka-yoke |

Bottlenecks can be minimized using the common Lean technique of *workload balancing*. This involves allocating work tasks so workers or other production resources are used as equally as possible. For example, if three workers are involved in carrying out a particular process, they should each be equally "busy" (utilized). This kind of balance leads to greater overall productivity, and it provides greater flexibility in adjusting to unforeseen circumstances.

*Layout/Facility Design*

Layout and facility design solutions relate to the physical environment in which work activities are performed. The 5S technique and the work cell are common Lean solutions for improving layout and facility design.

The *5S technique* is a systematic method consisting of sorting, straightening, scrubbing, standardizing, and sustaining. The technique is intended to create a more efficient organization of the physical workspace. A disorganized workplace will lead to excessive walking, processing, and other types of waste. In addition, disorganization can make it difficult to understand the current process and to envision possible improvements. Applying a 5S technique leads to an orderly and standardized workplace in which it is easy to detect abnormalities. Organizing the workplace also gives the work group a sense of ownership in its work space and processes. Figure 13 shows pictures of a before and after example.

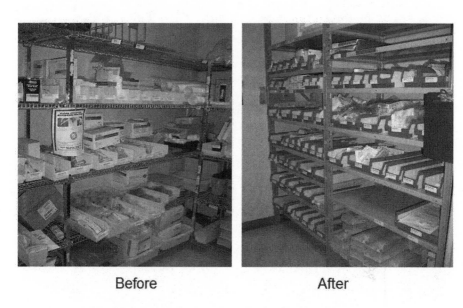

Before         After

Figure 13. Supply Shelf Before and After 5S Technique

A *work cell* is a physical arrangement of workers in which the workers are arranged in a U-shape, and the flow of work travels around the "U." This type of arrangement tends to reduce walking and motion waste. It also increases communication between the workers and allows for greater staffing flexibility. An example of a work cell is shown in Figure 14.

Figure 14. Work Cell
Courtesy: City Furniture

*Procedures/Methods*

Procedures and methods involve the nature and content of the actual work being performed. Common Lean solutions include batch size reduction and kitting.

Reducing the batch size can be an effective Lean solution because it improves the flow of the process and reduces waiting time and excessive inventory. Batch size reduction increases the number of process start-ups; therefore, this type of improvement will normally focus on "set-up activities" in order to reduce the time and effort required. In manufacturing, this set-up reduction is often described as "single minute exchange of die" or SMED. An example of set-up reduction in services might be to reduce the time and manpower required to organize files in preparation for paying a batch of invoices.

*Kitting* involves the use of a single package or "kit" of all the relevant materials, parts, and/or information needed to carry out a particular task. Kitting involves the building of appropriate kits and placing them at the point of use. This process will reduce the waste of walking for the process actor responsible for that task, but it will require some additional work in order to prepare and transport the kits. Kitting changes the procedure by replacing walking waste with easy, quick access to kits. An example of kitting often seen in the quick service restaurant industry is the staging of containers of lettuce, sliced tomatoes, and other vegetables in order to make lunch salads.

*Activity Sequence*

Lean solutions often focus on the sequence of activities in a process. This sequence change may include moving filtering activities to an earlier stage in the process to eliminate unnecessary work from later steps. It is also helpful to look for opportunities to adjust the process so activities previously carried out in sequence can be carried out in parallel. This will normally reduce total cycle time and related waiting times.

*Tools/Equipment/IT*

Finally, certain types of tools and equipment may be useful solutions. Common types described in this section include a kanban system, a kanban board, and a poka-yoke or fool-proof device.

In manufacturing, procurement, and other logistical processes, *kanban* is a tool for implementing pull. It is used primarily as a production scheduling method or reorder trigger in a procurement or supply chain application. In a production process, the kanban normally consists of a supermarket-type system in which the shelves are restocked as material is removed. The primary effect is to reduce excessive inventory and the associated wastes.

A simple example of a kanban system in a fast food restaurant is a "two-bin" system. With this type of system, when a grille person takes the last raw burger from the container, the container is set to the side. The runner takes the empty container to the back and exchanges it with a full container from the walk-in refrigerator.

Another type of kanban tool is a "kanban board." This is a useful tool commonly used in project management and *Agile* methodology. The board can be used to track the execution of a process, for example ordering office supplies. The columns might be generic progression indicators such as "to do," "doing," and "done," or they may be specific milestones associated with a particular process. The rows might indicate responsible individuals or groups of activities. Sticky notes or other markings may be used to track the progression of activities from left to right on the board. A sample layout for a kanban board is shown in Figure 15.

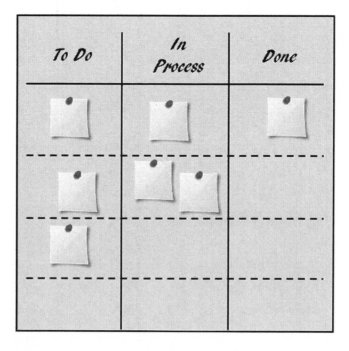

Figure 15. Kanban Board

A *poka-yoke* is a tool for preventing errors from occurring. Examples might include a microwave oven door, hospital wrist bands, a car that only starts in "park," or a pilot's checklist. In the case of the microwave oven door, the automatic shutoff feature is the poka-yoke, ensuring that harmful microwaves are not emitted when the door is open. The hospital wrist band is a type of poke-yoke because it can be used to ensure that patients receive the correct medication or are given the correct treatment. The key feature of a poka-yoke is that it is reasonably automatic and "foolproof."

# PART THREE

# CULTURE

# Chapter 8

# Surface Culture

"Never tell people how to do things.
Tell them what to do and they will surprise you with their ingenuity."
— General George Smith Patton, Jr.

IN THIS CHAPTER, the surface culture of a Lean system is described as a set of four management practices, which include goal-setting, empowering, partnering, and coaching. These practices provide a kind of "collaborative empowerment" environment that implements the third Lean principle of bottom-up management. While associates are intensively involved in the method, establishing and carrying out these management practices is the responsibility of organizational leaders.

For each practice, I explain its general purpose and how it is related to the Lean method and/or the other practices. I also briefly describe various, common Lean techniques (Liker 2004, Mann 2010) associated with each practice (see Table 6). Of course, this is not a complete list of Lean techniques. These particular techniques are presented to illustrate each general practice, and some of these techniques may not be necessary or even appropriate for your organization.

Table 6. Common Lean Techniques

| Management Practice | Lean Techniques |
|---|---|
| Goal-Setting | • Hoshin planning<br>• Lean event goals |
| Empowering | • Training within industry<br>• Suggestion systems<br>• Andon alerts |
| Partnering | • Kaizen teams and events<br>• Daily stand-up meetings<br>• A3 projects |
| Coaching | • Gemba walks<br>• Leader standard work |

## Goal-Setting

In the surface culture of a Lean organization, collaborative empowerment begins with the practice of goal-setting. This practice is necessary to provide a structure and guidelines in which empowerment can take place. Even though empowerment focuses on associates managing and improving the work, they still need to know how their work contributes to the organization's overall direction.

Goal-setting is a necessary and valuable practice in any organization. At the strategic level, companies typically establish goals for key performance indicators ("KPIs") that reflect the organization's most important metrics. Goals are also commonly set at the department and individual levels. It is often said that goals should be "SMART," meaning Specific, Measurable, Achievable, Relevant, and Time-bound (SMART criteria 2016).

Goals must be communicated in a clear and simple manner and in a way directly accessible by the associates. Goals should clearly lay out expectations and requirements, so associates can feel confident in accepting the responsibility that comes along with empowerment. In Lean literature, we sometimes refer to these as "stretch goals" to indicate that they should not be set so low that they are easy to reach, and yet they should not be set so high as to be clearly unattainable.

*Hoshin planning*

The Lean technique used for establishing strategic goals and plans is referred to as "hoshin planning."[28] This is a structured activity in which a "critical few" organizational goals and objectives are established. The hoshin planning activity is usually carried out on an annual cycle, and it often requires at least two or three months of activity, resulting in a finalized set of strategic objectives for the year. During the year, periodic reviews of progress measured against these goals are carried out to support accountability at all levels in the organization.

In a hoshin planning effort, the top leaders are primarily responsible for establishing strategic objectives. However, a significant level of involvement by other leaders and associates is sought through "catch-ball" activities. Catch-ball activities involve leaders drafting goals and strategies that are then circulated throughout the organization to obtain comments and feedback regarding the value of these proposed goals and the feasibility of the associated strategies.

Comments are then returned to the top leaders, who finalize the year's goals and objectives. This catch-ball feature is important because it shows the associates that their opinions are valued, and it increases the likelihood that they will buy in to and support the organization's strategic objectives.

---

28  Pronounced hoe'-shin.

*Lean Event Goals*

In comparison to traditional goals, which typically relate to a particular period such as a month, a quarter, or a year, the scope of a Lean event goal is focused on a particular Lean event.[29] These event goals are sometimes linked directly to hoshin planning objectives and the need for the event itself may have been identified during the hoshin planning effort. In some Lean events, the goals may be pre-set and defined in a project charter document. For other events, goals may be set informally or they may be reflected in a Lean vision for the process being assessed in the event.

## Empowering

> "Organizations learn only through individuals who learn."
> — Peter Senge

Empowering is the central practice of Lean's surface culture and the primary means for implementing the Lean principle of bottom-up management. The Lean method was built on the assumption that the people who actually do the work are the ones empowered to apply the method. These individuals have in-depth knowledge about how the work is performed,[30] and they are in the best position to visualize the process and identify areas of waste. Empowered workers are more likely to take "ownership" of the process and to sustain and even build upon the improvements they make.

Empowering must start with training to ensure that associates have the necessary knowledge and skills to apply the Lean method and to

---

29  Lean events such as kaizen events and A3 projects are described later in this chapter.

30  This type of knowledge is sometimes referred to as "tacit knowledge" (Polanyi 1966). Tacit knowledge is gained through experience but is difficult to explain to someone else. For example, you learn how to ride a bike by doing it rather than by someone telling you how to do it.

carry out their work. This requires training on the concepts, tools, and techniques of the method itself. Such training typically includes classes, access to training materials, and on-the-job training that occurs as part of the coaching practice. At a minimum, it is important that all associates learn how to recognize waste in their own surroundings and that they have a basic understanding of the concept of flow. At least some associates within each work group should also gain a working knowledge of visual controls, value stream mapping, and Lean solutions.

In addition to learning about the Lean method, training for empowerment also includes job-specific topics. For example, the roles and responsibilities for each position should be clearly documented to ensure that each associate and leader understands his or her own job and how it fits within the overall flow of work. Cross-training is often used to ensure that associates not only understand their own work but also how their work relates to other segments of the value stream. This practice further builds associates' knowledge and provides for maximum flexibility when making work assignments and reassignments.

### Training Within Industry

One of the most successful Lean techniques for training on job-specific topics is referred to as "Training Within Industry" (TWI). This technique was created during World War II and was then adapted by Toyota as it created its Toyota Production System (Dinero 2005). The technique fell out of favor but has been revived in recent years as a training method and as a means for spearheading Lean transformations.

TWI is a technique for "training the trainer." It supports a hands-on, mentoring style of training in which the trainer works closely with the trainee. The technique provides instructions to the trainer on how to establish the right atmosphere to minimize trainee anxiety and how to deal with mistakes by the trainee in a positive way. After the initial training session, TWI specifies the need for follow-up reviews by the trainer until the associate is fully confident with the procedure. Videos are also commonly used to provide guidance after the initial training session is completed, often as part of the visual controls readily accessible to all associates.

The key TWI document used in Lean training is the Job Breakdown Sheet. This sheet is carefully prepared by the trainer to reflect standard work and is used as a guide in teaching associates relevant procedures and skills.[31] The sheet lays out the important steps of the work, key points that can make or break the job and/or injure the worker, and the reasoning behind these steps and key points. Letting associates know the "why" behind the steps helps them to react to unexpected situations and to improve the work whenever possible.

*Suggestion Systems*

A suggestion system is another technique commonly used in Lean organizations to support the empowering practice. This type of system is important to ensure that associates feel they have an outlet for expressing their opinions and a uniform way of making improvement suggestions. This system might include the traditional "suggestion box" or, more commonly, a Lean organization will implement some type of open suggestion board with stick-on notes.

Regardless of the format in which suggestions are provided, it is important that the suggestion technique include a means for addressing the suggestion, perhaps assigning it to someone for follow-up, and then tracking it, and resolving it in some way. While not every suggestion is implemented, the important thing is that every suggestion is taken seriously and that the associate who provided the suggestion is treated with respect. A sure way to discourage future suggestions is to ignore or quickly dismiss the suggestions that have already been made.

31   Refer to Chapter 4, Standard Work.

*Andon Alerts*

In manufacturing, the andon alert technique is sometimes referred to as an "andon cord" where any worker on a production line can pull the cord and request immediate help if that worker sees a problem. After the andon alert is sounded, the problem that triggered the alert is immediately fixed, if possible. If the problem cannot be fixed immediately, the whole production line may be stopped. This ensures that the problem is not repeated and that the associates and customers do not have to wait for the correction/improvement to be made.

The andon alert technique can also be applied to a service environment. For example, any customer service associate at the Amazon call center can immediately remove an item from the Amazon website if that associate learns of a serious problem with the item during a customer call. Providing an andon alert option to an associate certainly emphasizes the word "power" in empowerment and makes the problem transparent, thus allowing for its quick resolution.

## Partnering

Partnering is another fundamental Lean system practice. In a partnering environment, associates actively work with and share information with others within their own department as well as with individuals in other departments. Associates work together in teams and are aware of, and focused on, the performance of the overall work process—not just their own particular tasks. With a partnering practice, the whole team is accountable for the team's overall performance, even though the frontline supervisor is ultimately accountable to upper-level management.

Partnering does not just involve associates. Rather, it involves associates who work together with leaders. In this context, partnering involves the practice of treating associates as partners, not individuals to be managed. On a departmental and individual level, this might involve employee councils, open discussion boards, and other efforts to foster collaborative and interdependent relationships between and among leaders and associates.

Typical Lean techniques for implementing a partnering practice include kaizen events, daily stand-up meetings, and A3 projects.

*Kaizen Events*

The most common organized venue for applying the Lean method is an event often referred to as a "kaizen event."[32] This event will normally be completed in five days or less, and many improvements are usually implemented within the time frame of the event. If the event is intended to produce significant changes, it is sometimes referred to as a "kaikaku event."

In a kaizen event, individuals participating in the Lean method are organized into teams, often referred to as "kaizen teams." A kaizen team includes process actors who are responsible for carrying out the process to be improved and managed. Because these processes often involve multiple functions and departments, the team will usually be cross-functional in nature and made up of team members representing the various relevant functional departments.

A kaizen team may include one or more specialists. These are individuals who have received specialized training and typically work on process improvement activities on a full-time basis, sometimes reporting to a program office. Leaders may also be involved in a kaizen event. However, both leaders and specialists will usually only play supportive roles. The process actors are the primary drivers of the team and the event.

---

32   Pronounced keye'zen.

*Daily Stand-Up Meetings*

Another common Lean technique for encouraging collaboration is the daily "stand-up meeting" or "huddle." This is a ten- or fifteen-minute meeting held every morning among members of a work group and their leader. It may be led by the group leader or by one or more associates, supported by visual controls. The meeting allows all associates to communicate with each other and with their leader about work from the previous day and plans for the current day. It is also an opportunity for associates to point out problem areas they may have noticed during the prior work day and to offer up ideas for improvement.

Figure 16. Daily Stand-Up Meeting
Courtesy: City Furniture

*A3 Projects*

Significant improvement events are sometimes referred to as "A3 projects."[33] This technique is used when in-depth planning and analysis is needed and implementation of improvements must be phased in over time. An A3 project usually begins with the development of a "project charter" document, and it may last from one to three months and even longer in some cases. As with the kaizen event, the A3 project is driven by process actors to the greatest extent possible. However, the project is often initiated by organizational leaders, and specialists may play a more active role because of the more complex nature of the problem and the types of solutions that need to be considered.

## Coaching

"Go see, ask why, show respect."

— Fujio Cho, Toyota Chairman

As a follow-up to empowerment and partnering, it is necessary for leaders to provide supportive mentoring and coaching to guide associates and teams as they carry out the Lean method. Coaching is conducted on a continual basis and requires frontline supervisors to be intimately involved with the daily performance of the work. This practice also requires a certain level of openness and a willingness on the part of leaders to release and share pertinent information.

Whenever possible, coaching involves asking questions of the associates and guiding them rather than micromanaging them. Allowing associates to think through problems and come up with answers on their own will take some time, but it is a necessary and valuable way of building their knowledge and capability to make improvements in the future. Associates won't learn as much if you give them the answer, and they

---

33   In Lean literature, the term "A3" is used in various ways, sometimes reflecting a certain type of thinking, a particular type of document, or a type of project. I use the term to reflect a type of project.

won't be as engaged or motivated to follow through with the answer. And, it is very possible that the "answer" provided by management is not even the best one anyway!

Coaching involves providing a certain amount of feedback on associate performance, although much of this type of information is obtained by associates directly from readily-accessible visual controls. In providing feedback, leaders need to react to both good and bad performance in a respectful and constructive way. Feedback should never be provided in a way that is openly disrespectful or purposefully embarrassing. Doing so is a sure way to damage trust and respect.

## Gemba Walks

In a Lean culture, coaching is usually conducted where the work is actually performed. In Lean literature, this place of work is referred to as the "gemba," and leaders are expected to carry out "gemba walks" where they "go to the gemba" and interact with the process actors performing the work. For example, the gemba might be the warehouse floor in a wholesale business or the service counter in a retail business. Leaders in a Lean culture are expected to visit these work places regularly so they can directly observe work activities and provide feedback and coaching.

## Leader Standard Work

Many Lean organizations use leader standard work. This is an explicit specification that communicates to leaders how they should spend their time. Leader standard work includes different types of activities and the percent of time that should be applied to each activity. At City Furniture, their leader standard work specifies that nearly 40 percent of a manager's time must be left open for working with his or her associates. This includes activities such as day-to-day coaching, training and development, recognizing and celebrating associate performance, and other supportive activities.

# Chapter 9

# Deep Culture

"If you treat people right they will treat you right…ninety percent of the time."

— Franklin D. Roosevelt

IN THE PREVIOUS chapter, the surface culture of Lean was described as a set of collaborative empowerment practices. These are observable activities that represent an essential component of the Lean system. In this chapter, I discuss the deep culture of Lean, which is reflected in the overall level of trust and respect that exists within the organization. While this aspect of a Lean culture is less visible than the surface culture, it is absolutely necessary if a Lean system is to flourish.

## Trust and Respect

The fourth fundamental principle of Lean supports the need for a culture of trust and respect, which is the foundation of any Lean system. A culture of trust and respect is the best way to maximize performance and, in the long run, is far more likely to succeed than one built on fear and intimidation. Mutual trust and respect within an organization is the glue that holds the entire Lean system together; a Lean system cannot function without a sufficient level of trust and respect.

Respect is basically an attitude I hold with respect to the value of another person that is reflected in certain types of behavior.[34] *Personal respect* reflects the extent to which I view another person as important and significant, merely because he or she is a human being. Stephen Covey, educator, entrepreneur, and author, refers to personal respect as recognizing the "intrinsic worth of individuals and...how you treat your fellow man, how you treat your team members, and how you treat your customers, your regulators, your general public, your audiences, your communities." (1989).

*Organizational respect* involves my assessment of your value to the organization. This assessment might include my respect for your competency, your effort, and/or your actual contribution. This is exhibited in behaviors showing that I recognize and appreciate your efforts and accomplishments.[35] Earning organizational respect means that I feel you are "credible." Organizational respect is specific to a particular task or role. My capability might be respected as a supervisor but not as an executive.

While respect is most commonly cited in the Lean literature, a Lean system actually emphasizes *both* trust and respect. The powerful effects of trust have been recognized in the general business literature, especially by Stephen M. R. Covey, son of Stephen Covey, in his book *The Speed of Trust* (2006). Trust, by itself, is critical to Lean culture and needs to be given the same consideration as respect.

Trust is essentially a perception or expectation that I hold about the intentions of another person in relation to me. At a basic level, my

---

34  Many features of personal respect are defined culturally. What is respectful behavior in one culture may be disrespectful in another.
35  Refer to Chapter 11, Recognition and Celebration.

trust in you reflects my perception that you will not try to harm me. At a higher level, my trust in you reflects my belief that you will keep my best interests in mind when you make decisions that might affect me. At the highest level, I believe that you care about me and I will expect you to take overt actions to help me whenever you can.

A person can earn my trust by consistently acting in a way that shows his or her positive intentions toward me. It can take weeks, months, even years to build up a relationship of trust. Unfortunately, one incident can cause an immediate and long-lasting loss of that trust.

Of trust and respect, respect is the most fundamental and important. It can be said that *personal respect is the platform upon which trust can grow.* However, trust may be viewed as more precious than respect because it takes longer to build, yet it is more fragile and can be destroyed in an instant.

At a personal level, our beliefs, perceptions, and attitudes will typically drive our behaviors,[36] and our perceptions and attitudes about trust and respect can have a powerful effect on our interactions with others. As you can see in Table 7, feeling trusted and respected can have important, positive effects, such as being open and willing to share information and having the desire to be with those who trust and respect us. It is also important to note that trust and respect tend to beget trust and respect. If I feel that you trust and respect me, then I am more likely to trust and respect you. This is the way in which mutual trust and respect are built.

In contrast, when associates do not feel respected or feel that they are not being treated fairly, they will tend to be apathetic, hoard information, and avoid responsibility or risk. They may do their jobs satisfactorily, but they definitely will not go the extra mile or fully apply their talents. In some cases, they may exhibit unproductive behaviors

---

36   Refer to Chapter 10, Worldview.

and may even sabotage the organization. If they don't trust their leaders and/or their peers, they will be distracted from doing their jobs. A lack of trust and respect will lead to suspicion and sometimes fear, which can result in a downward spiral in the overall level of trust and respect within the organization.

Table 7. Personal Reactions to Trust and Respect

| Personal reactions to feeling trusted/respected | Personal reactions to feeling distrusted/disrespected |
| --- | --- |
| If I feel trusted, I tend to … | If I feel distrusted, I tend to … |
| • Admit faults<br>• Take risks without fear of retribution<br>• Share information<br>• Trust those who trust me | • Hide my mistakes<br>• Avoid taking risks<br>• Hoard information<br>• Fear that person and shy away |
| If I feel respected, I tend to … | If I feel disrespected, I tend to … |
| • Trust the person who respects me<br>• Be willing to help that person<br>• Want to be with that person<br>• Act in a respectful manner | • Not trust that person<br>• Not want to help that person<br>• Ignore that person or even be hostile<br>• Stay away from that person |

In an organization, employees are most effective when they feel positively toward their jobs, leaders, and peers. They need to feel that their leaders respect and care about them. They need to feel listened to and trusted. They want to trust that the organization will provide fair compensation and an opportunity to develop and advance. When associates feel this way, most will behave in sustainably productive ways. They will tend to build lasting relationships, both within the organization and with customers, suppliers, and other stakeholders.

## Engagement

An organizational culture with a high level of mutual respect will lead to an environment of *engagement*. Engaged associates have energy and are willing to apply that energy toward advancing the organization's needs. These associates are committed to the organization and tend to be loyal and often joyful. They are proud of their organization and proud to be members of it. Cultures built on mutual respect will typically exhibit the features of engagement described in Table 8.

Table 8. Organizational Engagement

| Benefits | High Engagement | Low Engagement |
|---|---|---|
| Energy | • Passion<br>• Positive momentum<br>• Sometimes joyful<br>• High productivity | • Apathy<br>• Sluggishness<br>• Sometimes despairing<br>• Low productivity |
| Commitment | • Pride in organization<br>• Taking initiative<br>• Meeting expectations<br>• Low turnover<br>• Low absenteeism | • Disgust with organization<br>• Shirking responsibility<br>• Violating expectations<br>• High turnover<br>• High absenteeism |

In contrast, not feeling personal respect, and especially being subjected to abusive treatment, will cause associates to feel disengaged and to lose trust. This leads to high turnover and absenteeism, and in some cases, it may even lead to destructive behaviors or "active disengagement" such as sabotage (Fleming 2007). This is an incredible waste of human energy and creativity. The difference in performance between an organization with an engaged workforce and one with a disengaged workforce is enormous.

Engagement is an important facilitator of the Lean method itself. The likelihood that associates will actually apply themselves to seeking out continuous improvements (without someone looking over their shoulders) is much higher if these individuals are engaged. In addition, the highly-synchronized nature of Lean work will typically require a high level of attention and commitment from associates, which again is more likely if there is a high level of engagement.

### Transparency

"Our distrust is very expensive."
— Ralph Waldo Emerson

Mutual trust in an organization builds a general atmosphere of *transparency*. This condition means that there exists a general willingness to share information with others, a willingness to expose weakness in an attempt to improve, and a willingness to take risks. Cultures built on mutual trust will typically exhibit the features of organizational transparency as described in Table 9.

If a high level of mutual trust exists in an organization, associates are able to focus their attention and efforts on organizational purposes which, in a Lean system, will be directed toward producing value for customers. Covey (2006) describes this effect as the "speed of trust."

In contrast, a lack of mutual trust will produce a great deal of waste. Associates may waste an enormous amount of time and effort in covering their backs and forming coalitions, all activities that do not produce value for the customer! In addition, low levels of trust tend to require more controls such as audits and excessive quality control checks.

Transparency enhances the effectiveness of the Lean system because, in carrying out the coaching practice, leaders must make information available to their associates. This sharing of information is essential if the associates are expected to take a major role in improving and managing their own processes. At the same time, associates must be willing to reveal information about their process performance, which can sometimes involve admitting their own faults and mistakes.

Table 9. Organizational Transparency

| Benefits | High Transparency | Low Transparency |
|---|---|---|
| Focus | • Confidence<br>• Sharing information<br>• Candid communication<br>• True teamwork<br>• Streamlined controls<br>• High efficiency | • Fear<br>• Hoarding information<br>• Distorted communication<br>• Power games<br>• Extensive bureaucracy<br>• Low efficiency |
| Agility | • Innovation<br>• Taking risks<br>• Admitting faults<br>• Accepting change<br>• Adaptability | • Stagnation<br>• Avoiding risks<br>• Criticizing mistakes<br>• Fighting change<br>• Inflexibility |

# Chapter 10

# Personal Character

"Good character is not formed in a week or a month.
It is created little by little, day by day."
— Heraclitus of Ephesus

WHILE AN ORGANIZATION'S surface culture is made up of organizational practices and programs, its deep culture is built upon the
personal character of the leaders and associates who work within it. In
this chapter, I first discuss how values and character relate to our personal "worldview." I then reflect on personal character and the values
necessary to build a strong, deep Lean culture of trust and respect.

## Worldview

Character can be viewed as the set of values and beliefs that I hold
about the world around me and my place in that world. Covey (1989)
refers to these "below the surface" influencers of personal behavior as
"paradigms." They are also sometimes referred to as "worldview" (Koltko-Rivera 2004).

A worldview is an individual's deeply held beliefs and values. It is
what people really value and believe in. It is normally built up from early

childhood, is often invisible to others and even to oneself, and is extremely difficult to change. However, worldview is critically important because it drives personal behaviors. Worldview is the foundation for the personal character of any individual.

As seen in Figure 17, our worldview is the most influential factor in guiding our perceptions, attitudes, and, ultimately, our behavior. In his classic book, *The 7 Habits of Highly Effective People*, Covey explains that a change in our behavior requires changes to our perceptions, attitudes, and even to our fundamental values and beliefs (1989).

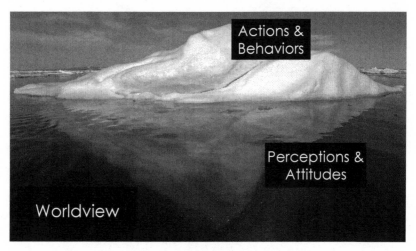

Figure 17. The Influence of Worldview

The key values needed to build trust and respect within a Lean system include accountability, integrity, respectfulness, and trustfulness. The values of accountability and integrity are norms that we hold ourselves to, and they are commonly described as valuable features of character. The values of respectfulness and trustfulness are beliefs that we hold about other people. These are not as commonly discussed, but they are just as important in a Lean system. Of these four values, accountability and respectfulness are focused on building mutual respect while integrity and trustfulness are focused on building mutual trust.

Each of these four values is discussed in the following sections, including a description of the types of behaviors normally associated with each value. In Chapter 11, I describe how these values relate to the behavior of leaders and why it is so important for both leaders and associates to hold these values.

## *Accountability*

Accountability is fully accepting responsibility for your own actions and for the outcomes of those actions. This does not mean that someone else holds you accountable. Rather, it means that you hold yourself accountable.

You take *responsibility* for your own actions. When things go wrong, you will not seek to blame others, but you will consider how much of the fault is your own. You will not avoid or shirk responsibility. You will take responsibility for results and consequences. You will not give excuses or try to explain away your lack of performance.

If you are accountable, you will keep your commitments. You will do what you say you will do. Therefore, you will be careful when making commitments to be sure you are not overpromising. If you are committed to holding information in confidence, then you will not break that commitment.

People who hold themselves accountable will deliver results. They will take responsibility for ensuring that they have the competency to carry out their responsibilities and will take constant steps to learn and improve themselves as much as possible. They will ensure that they are reliable in their performance and contribution to the organization.

## *Integrity*

Holding yourself to the norm of integrity means that you are honest, fair, and loyal. If you have integrity, you will not distort or manipulate the facts but will "tell it like it is." You will tend to use simple language and will not try to cloud the truth in ambiguous and complex communications.

Having integrity will lead you to be open and realistic in your dealings with others. When you can reasonably disclose important information, you will do so. You will not have hidden agendas and will present the truth even if it is painful. You will clearly state your expectations.

As a person of integrity, you will be fair in giving out credit and will show loyalty to others. You will not step on people or go behind their backs. You will speak about people in the same way whether they are present or not. You will not disclose private information about others.

## *Respectfulness*

The Lean value of respectfulness is a belief that it is important to *show* respect for others. This behavior is based on the belief that the person I am dealing with has value as a human being. This relates to the concept of personal respect and is separate from the concept of organizational respect, which is the extent to which I value your efforts, abilities, and contributions to the organization.

If I hold personal respect for you, I will act in a civil manner and will treat you with dignity. At a higher level, personal respect means that I will show you consideration and that I actually care about your well-being. I will be empathetic, kind, and will take the time to listen to what you have to say. If I hold this value, then the people around me will feel the respect I have for them. If I offer water to a service worker who is working at my house, that is a way of showing respect and caring.

A respectful person will tend to be humble, not egotistical. He or she will not show false pride and be unwilling to admit fault. They will recognize that it is okay to be wrong at times, they will admit when they are wrong, and they will want to explain their actions without trying to make excuses. They will take action to correct the situation.

With respectful behavior, it is usually the "little things" that can make a big difference. This might involve a nod of acknowledgment, a short note or email, a tone of voice, a smile, or even just saying hello and remembering someone's name. If you firmly believe in the value of respectfulness, these small actions will be practiced regardless of the status and position of the person you are dealing with.

In contrast with these positive behaviors, a lack of respectfulness will be reflected in disrespectful and even abusive behaviors. Disrespectful behaviors can range from more moderate examples such as shunning or not saying hello, to more serious examples such as:

> ...belittling the abilities and competency of another, constantly criticizing, being insulting or calling names, refusing to communicate, manipulating, causing guilt feelings, intimidating, threatening physical harm, making unfounded accusations, and destroying property. (Covey 2006, p. 148)

## *Trustfulness*

Trustfulness means that you are willing to extend trust to others and give them the benefit of the doubt. The value of trustfulness is that it is a *show* of trust toward others. Being trustful will lead others to feel that you trust them.

A person who values trustfulness will not be overly skeptical and will want to extend trust to others. He or she will recognize trustworthy behavior in others and will extend trust accordingly. A trustful leader will not want to micromanage his or her associates. A trustful person will assume good intentions and will look for the value in others. He or she will be generally optimistic about the intentions, willingness, and capabilities of others.

However, this does not mean that you trust everyone. You have a belief in others' trustworthiness, but it is not a blind belief. Trustful people will start relationships with measured trust by giving the benefit of the doubt. They will not assume that others are untrustworthy, but they will also be vigilant to see whether their trust is earned as time goes on.

# Chapter 11

# The Lean Leader

"The only thing of real importance that leaders do is to create and manage culture."

— Edgar Schein, Professor and Author of
*Organizational Culture and Leadership* (2010).

THE PRIMARY JOB of the leader is to build and maintain the culture. This involves his or her personal behavior and interactions as well as the ways in which he or she establishes organizational policies, especially with regard to human resource practices. Organizational policies and practices need to show respect and build trust. The Lean leader must be the primary change agent and cultural steward. He or she must take the lead in building the culture, changing the thinking when needed, and finding and retaining employees whose character is consistent with the changing culture.

## *Personal Behavior*

"It is amazing what you can accomplish if you do not care who gets the credit."

— Harry S. Truman

The most important factor in building a Lean culture is that leaders possess and practice the Lean values discussed in the previous chapter. This is especially true for frontline supervisors because they have the greatest influence on associate engagement. Leaders must practice the Lean values and reflect these values in their management style. They must set a personal example in this regard.

## Accountability

Leaders must hold themselves accountable if associates are to respect them. Leaders must earn organizational respect and should not expect that merely holding a position title is enough to gain respect. Associates must believe that their leaders are capable of carrying out their leadership roles. In effect, the leader must have credibility.

The leader must challenge others to be accountable for improving their own performance and the performance of their team. It is important to recognize that the best approach is to get associates to hold themselves accountable rather than having to hold them accountable. This can be facilitated by a leader who gives fair recognition of accomplishments. Recognition can reinforce associates who take responsibility for their own actions, and withholding recognition can discourage associates who make excuses.

A fascinating discussion of accountability is included in Jim Collins' book *Good to Great* (Collins 2001). In this book, Collins presents the results of extensive research conducted to identify commonalities among firms that were in the middle of the pack and then became great, far outperforming competitors over an extended period of time.

Among the significant factors identified were certain characteristics among the CEOs of these great firms. Surprisingly, these firms were not led by charismatic, outgoing individuals. Rather, the CEOs were quite humble and, in particular, clearly held themselves accountable for their own actions. Collins describes the attitudes of these CEOs as reflecting "a window and a mirror"—when things go well, they look out through the window to others; when things go poorly, they look into the mirror at themselves.

*Integrity*

A leader must have the highest level of integrity in order to elicit trust from others. It is important that all associates trust their leader's intentions. Leaders should not just talk about integrity. They must practice what they preach.

A leader with integrity will maintain a consistent message. Changing your position on key matters without explanation and/or saying different things to different people will be viewed as hypocritical and is a sure sign of a lack of integrity.

If associates believe that their leader lacks integrity, they will tend to lose respect and become distrustful and disengaged. Of course, associates must also have integrity, and a leader must be prepared to deal firmly with individuals who do not.

*Respectfulness*

Showing personal respect is the *foundation* for building a culture of trust and respect. Without this type of behavior, the rest of the values and behaviors are irrelevant. It is very difficult to trust a leader who does not respect you, especially if you feel that person does not care about you. To elicit trust from associates, a leader must first be respectful toward them.

The most important type of respectfulness is the extent to which the leader *truly cares* about his or her associates, both as employees and as people. A leader who cares about associates will take an interest in their development and will look for opportunities for them to grow and advance. If associates believe their leader really cares about them, they tend to be highly engaged and may even be willing to forgive some negative behaviors.

Fairness is also critical, especially with regard to recognition and celebration. Respectful and caring leaders look for the value in others and eagerly give them credit and recognition. They will want to show their appreciation and gratitude for associates' work. However, they will only give credit when credit is due and will not give it when it is not earned.

It is important to realize that a respectful leader is not necessarily "nice." In fact, the most effective leaders tend to be demanding and to hold others accountable if they are not holding themselves accountable. Collins' work shows that great leaders are humble but highly committed to their organization and that they are demanding but in a respectful way (Collins 2001).

### Trustfulness

Leaders must be willing to extend trust. This is important because to build a culture of mutual respect and trust, associates must feel that their leaders trust their intentions and capabilities.

As noted by Covey (2006), a "high-trust" leader must:

> Demonstrate a propensity to trust. Extend trust abundantly to those who have earned your trust. Extend trust conditionally to those who are earning your trust. Learn how to appropriately extend trust to others based on the situation, risk, and credibility (character and competence) of the people involved. But have a propensity to trust. Don't withhold trust because there is risk involved. (Covey 2006, p. 229)

McGregor's work (1960) regarding what he refers to as "Theory X" and "Theory Y" offers insight into the importance of trustfulness. McGregor suggested that managers can hold different types of beliefs about their workers. A manager with a Theory X belief assumes that most employees are basically lazy and not sincerely interested in doing a good job. In contrast, a manager who believes in Theory Y feels that most people actually want to do a good job and that they just need to be challenged and treated properly. McGregor argued that the most effective managers follow Theory Y.

Since McGregor's time, it has been observed that the manger's beliefs can have a significant effect on the behavior of associates (Schein 2010). In particular, a cynical leader who holds a Theory X belief and acts in a highly suspicious manner toward associates can actually influence some individuals to become disengaged and even to act in an untrustworthy manner. In a downward spiral, this behavior can reinforce the leader's assumption that these associates are not trustworthy.

In comparison, a leader with a Theory Y belief who gives the benefit of the doubt is more likely to bring about the trustworthy behavior in associates. In some cases, showing confidence and belief in associates may lead them to perform at a higher level than even they thought possible. This can happen when leaders look for the potential in employees, rather than focusing on weaknesses and failures.

Of course, there are some people who simply cannot be trusted. As Covey (2006) notes, the extension of trust must be conditional. It is okay to give the benefit of the doubt, but start with little extensions of trust, and verify that that trust is being honored. Thus, Lean leaders would be well advised to follow the philosophy of "Theory Y but verify!"

*Reflections*

As a leader, it is important not to become caught up in daily activities and to reflect on your own values and behaviors. The best leaders create an atmosphere that people like to work in. They coach, they challenge, and they empower others. They are curious. They are hands-on and supportive. They are capable of having empathy. They are self-confident, open, and not hypocritical. As a leader, which of these traits do you think applies to you, and which do you think may not?

It is necessary for leaders to be close to their associates and to their work. A leader needs to be close in order to build and extend trust and to provide fair and appropriate recognition. Are you close enough to the work? How much time do you actually spend "at the gemba," the place where the work is being performed? Are you close enough to your associates and their work to feel comfortable in extending them trust and providing fair recognition? One of the most damaging situations occurs when a leader frequently acknowledges an associate who is not providing the most value and contribution.

A leader may try to exhibit certain behaviors, but these behaviors will seem artificial and "counterfeit" if they are not consistent with his or her deeply held values and beliefs (Covey 2006). Without a sincere belief in what you are doing, it often becomes obvious that you are merely "going through the motions." For example, without a solid grounding in personal values, the practices of collaborative empowerment may appear hollow and actually be counterproductive in their effect on trust and respect. Do you truly believe in the way you deal with your associates, or do you sometimes just go through the motions?

Of course, the four Lean values are not a complete recipe for success and an effective leader must possess many other traits. In addition, these values do not represent a definitive litmus test for a Lean leader. No one is perfect, and it can be difficult to fully follow all of these values, all of the time. In reality, each leader will bring his or her own unique style to the organization and the most effective Lean leaders will strive to incorporate these values into their styles to the greatest extent possible.

## Recognition and Celebration

Leaders must be very aware of the performance and contribution of their associates and must ensure that proper organizational programs and practices are in place so that associates feel their work is recognized and appreciated. These programs include the rates and structures of compensation and benefits, financial and non-financial incentives, and other awards and events.

### Compensation and Benefits

Compensation programs should be as generous as possible given the nature of the industry, the region, and the financial situation of the organization. If possible, compensation should include provisions for all employees to share in the company's financial success—through stock options and/or profit sharing plans, for example. Paying employees at or below the average market rate tells them the organization does not respect them, provided, of course, the company has sufficient financial resources to pay higher rates.

Employee benefit programs should show that the organization cares about its people and their families. These programs normally include traditional health and life insurance, disability income protection, vacation and sick leave, and retirement benefits. Lean organizations will add various services and amenities such as daycare, health classes, and other specialized benefits.

### Incentives, Awards, and Events

Incentives are important both in acknowledging employee contributions and as a means for reinforcing desired behaviors. In order to align properly with the goals of a Lean system, incentive programs should emphasize performance gains rather than performance levels. While individual incentives have their place, an emphasis should be placed on group incentives that encourage teamwork by focusing on team performance and knowledge-based incentives, which encourage learning and cross-training. In addition, KPI-based incentives should be reviewed to ensure that they are not in conflict with Lean thinking.

Incentives may be financial or non-financial. Financial rewards are most effective when provided in combination with intrinsic rewards that are more personal in nature (Pink 2009). Intrinsic rewards may involve organized award programs, celebrations and/or recognition events. Financial rewards are certainly important, but they do not generally lead to engagement. However, a lack of appropriate financial reward can certainly cause disengagement.

No contribution should be considered too insignificant for recognition and celebration. However, it is important that the extent of the recognition matches the extent of the contribution. Successful Lean leaders are always looking for ways to celebrate their employees' accomplishments. These might include banners, videos, recognition walls (see Figure 18), and other forms of celebration. The traditional birthday and/or anniversary celebrations are also a typical part of the mix. However, it is important that these celebrations are sincere expressions of appreciation and that they do not become "robotic."

### Human Resource Practices

In addition to recognition and celebration programs, various other human resource programs and practices, while not directly related to a Lean system, are certainly important in supporting a Lean system. These include employment practices, training and development, organizational design, and work scheduling.

Figure 18. Group Recognition Wall
Courtesy: City Furniture

*Employment Practices*

Employment practices in a Lean organization should explicitly seek out people who possess and exhibit Lean values. In recruiting for a Lean organization, it is generally best to hire on character and train skills. However, identifying a person's character can be difficult because this aspect of a candidate is complex and as individual as his or her fingerprint. To assist in this effort, consider using screening tests and role-playing exercises that may help to uncover an applicant's character.

With regard to existing personnel, leaders must be prepared to release individuals who have poor character and are unable or unwilling to change. Employee termination can be an especially difficult decision if an employee is a high performer in some ways but shows a serious lack of character in one or more of the Lean values. However, building the right culture is critical to the Lean system's success and obstacles to the culture must be removed.

In a Lean transformation, there are usually some individuals who have a great deal of difficulty in adjusting to the Lean way of thinking. If they have a positive attitude and character, a leader should be patient with these individuals as they struggle with the challenge of thinking in new ways. Sometimes individuals will eventually need to be released. However, leaders should be prudent and show restraint when making such decisions, keeping in mind the need to respect the terminated individual while continuing to build trust and respect among the entire workforce.

## Training and Development

As discussed in Chapter 8, training is a critical element if associates are to be fully empowered. In that chapter, I discussed process training using the Training Within Industry method. However, in addition to process-specific areas, training should also extend to other areas that help build an employee's knowledge. Training of both leaders and associates might relate to organizationally-specific areas, or it may pertain to more general areas that support the individual's career and/or personal development.

In career development, one of the best ways to show respect for an employee is to lay out a well-defined career path providing ample opportunity for advancement, both professionally and financially. This practice often works hand in hand with a "promote from within" policy. It can also include broader development programs encouraging employees to obtain certifications and to expand their professional knowledge in a way that builds their confidence and adds to their capabilities.

## Organizational Design and Work Scheduling

In some respects, the empowerment aspect of the Lean system may seem to require a "flat organization" with few layers of management. However, the need for leaders to work very closely with associates leads to an organizational design that has a limited span of control resulting in multiple layers. For example, City Furniture targets a seven-to-one associate-to-leader ratio that makes it possible for leaders to spend up to half of their time working directly with their associates.

In a Lean organization, job descriptions tend to be broad and job rotation and job sharing is common. This type of design supports broader knowledge among associates and is very useful in supporting the tightly-synchronized work patterns associated with flow. In addition, work scheduling should be as flexible as possible, showing consideration for the individual's home life and recognizing the importance of work-life balance.

# PART FOUR

# LEARN BY DOING

# Chapter 12

# Lean 7-Step Process Improvement Method

THIS PART OF the book contains a 7-step process improvement method that can be used by any type or size organization as it makes its first attempt at conducting a Lean improvement event.[37] For example, this approach could be useful when organizing a kaizen team to carry out its first kaizen event. Of course, this would only apply if the organization did not already have a well-established Lean improvement method.

The method includes practical tools and instructions designed to be useful for improving any type of stable[38] work process. This excludes one-time activities which are really "projects" and not processes. For these types of activities, managers should consider using Scrum or other types of project management methods as described in Chapter 2.

The seven steps of the method are listed in Table 10 and are described in the following sections. Step 1 includes scoping the process under con-

---

37   Further details and tool templates can be found at www.essenceoflean.com.
38   An unstable process is one that changes significantly each time it is executed (refer to Chapter 4, Process View). A process must be stabilized before applying the Lean 7-Step method.

sideration and identifying process stakeholders to be interviewed during the event. In Step 2, the scoped "target process" is studied in detail and mapped out using facts and data obtained by observing the current process. This can be thought of as visualizing the "current situation."

Table 10. Lean 7-Step Process Improvement Method

| Step Description | Deliverable |
|---|---|
| Step 1: Scope the process and identify stakeholders | Canvas column 1 |
| Step 2: Describe and map the process | Value stream map |
| Step 3: Assess value and process performance | Canvas column 2 |
| Step 4: Identify points of waste and root causes | Canvas column 3 |
| Step 5: Formulate a Lean vision | Lean vision statement |
| Step 6: Evaluate and select improvements | List of solutions |
| Step 7: Standardize the improvements | Canvas column 4, Standard work guide, Visual controls |

In Step 3, the team uses observations from Steps 1 and 2 to assess the types of value required by process stakeholders and the current level of process performance as perceived by those stakeholders. These assessments must be based on the perceptions of the process stakeholders and should not reflect the individual opinions of kaizen team members.

Problem definition and problem-solving activities are carried out in Steps 4, 5, and 6. In the Lean method, waste is viewed as the problem and recognizing waste is the way in which the problem is defined. During these steps, various possible changes are envisioned and then experiments are performed and evaluated to solve the waste problem.

In Step 7, selected improvements are implemented and systematized. They become part of the organization's operating system, which involves the development of standard work guides and the implementation of visual controls that provide clear and rapid feedback to associates regarding the status and performance of their processes. The standard work guide also provides a foundation for continuing the learning cycle of the Lean method after the event is finished.

> *Remember to involve the process actors as much as possible. The key is that they start to feel ownership and become engaged in continuously learning and improving.*

On your first attempt at Lean improvement, you should follow each step. However, if you feel some parts of the method could be improved and/or other ways would work better for your organization, then try them! This method is just a starting point. As you apply these steps, you will learn about the process you are studying. But you will also learn about the method itself and how it is best applied in your organization.

> *In making your first attempt, the key is to just go ahead and do something. Don't expect to understand every step in full or to do everything "correctly." The more you do, the better you will get.*

### Lean Event Canvas

While the seven steps are meant to be completed in sequence, the team should realize there is often a need to loop back and make adjustments to the results of previous steps. In order to help keep the kaizen team on track during the event, a "Lean Event Canvas" is provided on

Figure 19. The canvas can be helpful in keeping track of changes and loop-backs during the event. It can also help to clarify the logical flow of the event (see Figure 20) and can be used after the project is completed as a summary presentation of the project and its results.

In the following sections, relevant chapters and sections of Part Two are referenced in each step. At the end of each step, a list of questions to be answered by the kaizen team is provided. In addition, each step is illustrated using an example of how the method was actually applied at XSolutions Consulting Services, LLC, a computer software and services company based in New York. The XSolutions case study is described below.

### XSolutions Case Study

XSolutions Consulting Services, LLC is a computer technology firm offering a range of services including computer support, cloud services, business intelligence, and IT consulting. The company is owned and operated by Joseph Imperato, Jr. and his father, Joseph Imperato, Sr. Client services are provided by a number of local and remote technical specialists ("Techs"), a Network Operations Center, and other partner service providers, under the supervision of an Operations Manager ("Ops Mgr") and a Technical Manager ("Tech Mgr"). The computer support function involves a managed IT services program where XSolutions provides full hardware and software support to small- and medium-size businesses.

Various types of requests for service can be made by a managed IT services client. These requests range from simple questions about how to open a program to more serious issues such as a computer crash. The receipt of a request for service triggers the creation of a support ticket and a process in which the request is addressed in the most expeditious manner. While this support ticket handling process seems to be working quite well from the client's point of view, XSolutions is growing rapidly and company executives want to improve the productivity of the process and ensure that their high level of service continues in the future.

As a result, the owners organized a kaizen team and carried out a kaizen event for the purpose of applying the 7-Step Lean process improvement method to the support ticket handling process. Because of time and schedule limitations, the event was carried out in stages during available off-hour times and so it required a total of about 3 weeks to complete. Remotely based employees were included via teleconferencing. The Lean Event Canvas was used throughout.

After the event was completed, Joseph Imperato, Jr. reflected on the results: "While we had dabbled with Lean in the past, this was our first attempt at a formal kaizen event. Working the event into our busy schedule was not easy, but it turned out to be well worth the effort. We wanted to improve the efficiency and productivity of the process, and we certainly did that. At the same time, we also improved the quality of the process as perceived by our customers by recognizing and responding to the client's need for greater communication. Basically, we are now better serving our client's needs, and yet we are using fewer resources!"

"However, I believe the greatest impact of this event was how it affected our thinking and motivation. We now seem to be spending more time thinking in depth about customers and asking what they really want and need in many different situations. We also feel that we have a better understanding of the ticket handling process, and we are excited to continue learning about the process and how we can make it better and better. The event really helped us to realize what continual learning is all about and how critical this kind of learning can be to our future growth and success."

# Lean Event Canvas for (process name)

| Steps 1-2 Process, Stakeholders | Step 3 Value, Performance | | Step 4 Points of Waste | Steps 5-7 Vision, Improvements |
|---|---|---|---|---|
| | Value Factors | Performance Grades | | |
| Process Outputs: | Quality: | Quality: | Defects: | Lean Vision: |
| Process Customers: | Speed: | Speed: | Waiting: | Immediate Actions: |
| Process Milestones: | Productivity: | Productivity: | Overproduction: | Scheduled Actions: |
| Process Actors: | Compliance: | Compliance: | Non-productive Activities: | Future Possible Actions: |
| Organizational Agents; | | | | |

Figure 19. Lean Event Canvas

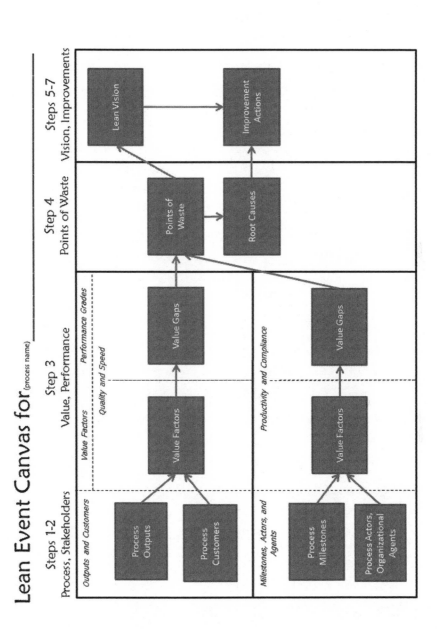

Figure 20. Logical Flow of the Lean Event

### *Step 1: Scope the Process and Identify Stakeholders*[39]

The team first defines the process scope and identifies key process stakeholders. This identifying is done so that the kaizen team clearly understands *what* is to be studied during the event and *who* the key players are—who needs to be considered and/or contacted. The process to be studied is referred to as the "target process."

The scope is a statement of the starting and ending points of the process to be studied, along with key milestones that occur during the process. The milestones define logical segments of the process between one milestone and another. The beginning or trigger of the process is always the first milestone, and the last activity in the process is the last milestone. One or more additional milestone points may then be defined.

In this step, it is not necessary (or even desirable) to list every single activity in the target process. You should provide just enough detail to be sure that the team has a good understanding of the boundaries and key parts of the process to be studied. This would include the starting and ending milestones and perhaps two or three intermediate milestones. The full detail of the process will be explored in Step 2.

> *When scoping a process, it is useful to first choose an ending point and to identify the process outputs. Then you can identify an appropriate starting point and think through the activities and milestones necessary to move from the starting point to the ending point.*

A process' boundaries are defined by its starting and ending points. If a different chunk of work is desired, then it is merely necessary to

---

39   Refer to Chapter 4, Process View and Chapter 5, Process Stakeholders.

change either of those two points and a new process can be defined. The level of aggregation of a process is also a matter of choice.

Sometimes, an event can undergo "scope creep," where the boundaries of the target process change as the event proceeds. Such changes may be necessary and useful in some situations, but changes in scope should be identified early. Having a clear definition of the process' scope on the front end will help the team track scope changes and ensure the whole team understands exactly what activities are being studied.

For XSolutions, the triggering milestone was agreed to be *the initial customer contact,* and the ending milestone was *documenting the ticket* (after the ticket work is completed). Two intermediate milestones were defined to include *opening and assigning the ticket* and *fixing the issue (satisfying the request).* The name of the process was defined as "Support Ticket Handling."

## How to Define the Right Process Scope

Defining a process is a matter of choice. The process scope should be broad enough to include most of the activities that have an influence on the outputs. For example, the scope of a payroll process should include all of the payroll activities that affect the quality and timeliness of the primary output, which is a paycheck. However, the scoped process should not be so extensive as to provide an overwhelming challenge for the kaizen team during a single Lean event.

The use of process outputs should be included in the scope so the effectiveness of process activities in producing value for output users (process customers) can be properly assessed. For example, the scope of an order-taking process should incorporate the final receipt and acceptance of the order by the customer and should not be ended at the point where the goods are shipped to the customer.

In order to address a particular goal or problem, it is necessary to scope out a process that is having a direct effect on that problem. For example, a manager perceived that her restaurant had a problem with excessive labor costs because these costs, expressed as a percentage of sales, were higher than the industry average. Organizing a Lean event to address the goal of reducing labor costs required that a process be identified that significantly contributed to labor costs. The majority of labor costs were associated with the front-of-house and back-of-house personnel who served the patrons. Therefore, the process scope chosen included serving patrons from the time they entered the restaurant until the table was cleaned.

At XSolutions, they realized a number of variations existed in the ticket handling process. Sometimes, the customer initiated the process, but sometimes, it was automatically triggered by software. In addition, some situations required escalation to higher level technical resources and/or the use of the Network Operations Center (NOC). For this kaizen event, the target process scope was limited to include only customer-initiated tickets that do not require escalation. (More complex process variations were set aside to be addressed in the future in the course of continuous learning.)

### Identifying Stakeholders

Three primary types of process stakeholders are the most important: process customers, process actors, and organizational agents. These stakeholders are identified in the first step of the event because they will either be contacted or explicitly considered at some point during the event. In particular, process customers and organizational agents are primary sources for identifying value and performance assessments in Step 3. The process actors provide information about the process itself and are also involved in identifying and evaluating improvements.

The process customers are the primary users of the target process outputs. These process customers may be individuals who are traditionally viewed as regular customers of the organization ("paying customers" or "external customers"), or they may be "internal customers" such as employees or business partners. For example, the process customers for a payroll process would be employees who receive a paycheck as an output of that process.

Process actors actually carry out the process to be improved. These individuals are usually associates of the organization, although external customers and suppliers may also be process actors in a service process. Leaders may also function as process actors.

Organizational agents are the individuals who represent the organization's interests. These individuals typically include owners, directors, executives, and/or managers who act as agents of the organization. In order to keep the event manageable, it can be assumed that organizational agents also represent the interests of the process actors and other stakeholders such as regulatory agencies.

There may be other stakeholders who should be recognized even though they are not directly involved in the event. If the process customers are not the external or paying customers, then those individuals should be explicitly considered as "other stakeholders." Internal actors and groups who may be affected by changes to the target process should also be recognized as other stakeholders.

The process scope and stakeholder information for the XSolutions process is summarized on Figure 21. This figure illustrates how Lean Event Canvas entries are made using bullet points and/or brief statements.

| Process Name: | Process Milestones: |
|---|---|
| Support Ticket Handling | • Initial customer contact |
| | • Create ticket |
| **Process Outputs:** | • Fix issue |
| • Support request satisfied | • Document ticket |
| • Documentation completed | |
| | **Process Actors:** |
| **Process Customers:** | • Techs |
| • Clients under contract | • Ops Mgr |
| • Ops Mgr (administrative use of documentation) | **Organizational Agents:** |
| • Tech Mgr (technical use of documentation) | • Owners |

Figure 21. Lean Event Canvas Entries for
Column 1 (Step 1): Process, Stakeholders

*Step 1 Questions:*

1) What are the starting and ending points for the target process?

2) What are the key milestone points between the starting and ending points?

3) What is a short but descriptive name for the process?

4) What are the primary outputs of the process?

5) Who are the process customers (the primary users of the process outputs)?

6) Who are the process actors (that actually carry out the process)?

7) Who are the organizational agents that look after the organization's interests for this process?

## Step 2: Describe and Map the Process[40]

This step involves extensive observation such as interviewing personnel, reviewing procedure manuals, forms, and other process documents, watching operations, and otherwise collecting information about the target process. Special emphasis should be given to actually observing the process in action. Recording your observations with photos or videos can be very helpful. This step should focus on the process *as it is currently practiced* and not how it is "supposed to be practiced" or how the team thinks it should be practiced.

This step involves "visualizing" the process itself both physically and mentally. It includes extensive data collection regarding the details of the process activities, their sequence, and any metrics that may be relevant to the process. In identifying this information, it is critical to interview and observe the process actors who actually carry out the target process on a day-to-day basis. Of course, the kaizen team will normally include a number of these process actors.

The primary tool for documenting the details of the target process is a value stream map. The value stream map is essential for understanding the process itself. It is also used as a reference in later steps for the team to recognize points of waste and to envision actions that could lead to improved flow.

A value stream map depicts target process activities and their sequence, and it includes activity metrics that are useful to the team in visualizing the various activities in the process. These might include metrics such as activity time, wait time, percent defects, volume, labor required, and/or distance travelled. The activity metrics included on the value stream map are not the same as process performance metrics, which are discussed in Step 3. Activity metrics refer to individual activities while process metrics refer to the overall process and its status or performance.

40    Refer to Chapter 4, Visual Mapping.

The most important metric on a value stream map is time. The two primary time metrics include activity time and wait time. Activity time is the actual time required to conduct each activity. This is the time during which activities are being performed on material, information, or a served person. Wait time is the time that typically elapses between the end of one activity and the beginning of another. This includes time while material, information, or the served person is idle, for example, in a queue or in storage. This is the time between activities when "nothing is happening." Wait time also includes downtime, which delays the completion of an ongoing activity.

While much of the Lean literature refers to a standard form for a value stream map (Rother and Shook 2003), this standard form is most relevant to "linear" processes in manufacturing or supply chains. Service processes tend to be more network (or non-linear) shaped with many feedback loops (Fitzsimmons & Fitzsimmons 2014). Therefore, a more universal technique for value stream mapping is suggested, which is intended to be useful for all types of processes. This version of a value stream map is made up of three different documents that include a value stream flowchart, a process details table, and a Gantt chart.

On a value stream flowchart, the activities are represented by boxes and their interactions are represented by arrows that connect the boxes. An arrow connecting Box A to Box B indicates that Activity A must be completed before Activity B can begin. An example of a value stream flowchart for the XSolutions support ticket handling process is shown in Figure 22.

On the figure, the activity boxes are separated into four columns, corresponding to activities conducted by the client, the Tech, the Operations Manager ("Ops Mgr"), and the automated systems. This "swim lane" technique is often useful but not required. Rectangles are used for general activities and diamonds are used for decision activities.

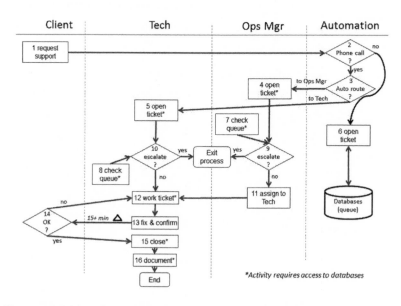

Figure 22. Value Stream Flowchart, Support Ticket Handling Process

As seen on the figure, the support ticket handling process includes 16 activities or steps. The process is started by a request from a client for support (step 1) and it finishes when the internal documentation is completed (step 16). The two primary outputs of this process are the satisfaction of the support request (step 13) and the production of the internal documentation (step 16).

If the client request is received via a phone call, the automated phone system automatically routes the call to either the Ops Mgr or an available Tech (step 3) and either the Ops Mgr or the Tech will open the ticket (step 4 or 5). If the request is received electronically, the ticket is opened automatically by the system (step 6). For these automatically opened tickets, the Ops Mgr and the Techs check the queue screen in the system about every 10 minutes to see whether an unassigned ticket needs to be assigned (steps 7 and 8).

Once a ticket is opened, a decision is made whether or not to escalate it beyond the Tech to the Tech Mgr (steps 9 and 10). If the ticket is escalated, then other activities occur that are outside the scope of the target process (i.e., these other activities are not assessed in detail during this event). If the ticket is not escalated, then it is assigned by the Ops Mgr to a Tech (step 11) or, if already assigned, it is worked by the assigned Tech (step 12).

After the request is satisfied and the issue is "fixed," the Tech calls the client to confirm that the client is satisfied with the fix (step 13). If the client is not available at that time, the Tech waits for the client to call back. This waiting time often requires 15 minutes or more, as noted on the flowchart. If the client requires further work, the Tech continues to work the ticket. If the client is satisfied, the ticket is closed and the Tech completes the internal documentation of the ticket.

While metrics may sometimes be shown directly on the value stream flowchart, it is recommended that these details be kept on the process details table in order to keep the flowchart uncluttered. Table 11 illustrates a sample process details table for the target process. The team decided to capture three activity metrics, including activity time, average daily volume, and percent defects. In the example, activity times are listed on the table and key wait times are shown directly on the flowchart. A column for defects was incorporated, but no significant defects were observed during the event. However, the column was retained as a reminder to search continually for defect waste. Note that the activity time listed should be the approximate time required to complete that activity *for a typical batch*. (The typical batch size should be noted.)

To understand and visualize the process in full, it is also necessary to prepare an associated Gantt chart. As seen in Figure 23, each activity in the target process is represented by a horizontal bar on the chart. Each bar is placed so that it begins only after preceding activities are completed. Note that the length of each bar roughly corresponds to the actual time required to complete an activity ("activity time"), and this length *does not* include any waiting or downtime that may occur either before, during, or after this activity is completed. The chart is intended to give a general visual impression of the sequencing and portion of time required for each activity. Therefore, exact precision in the length of each bar is not necessary.

Table 11. Process Details Table, Support Ticket Handling Process

| Activity | Activity Time | Volume | Defect % |
|---|---|---|---|
| 1. request support | 5 min | 10/day | |
| 2. phone call? | | | |
| 3. auto route? | 1 min | | |
| 4. open ticket (Ops Mgr) | 5 min | | |
| 5. open ticket (Tech) | 5 min | | |
| 6. open ticket (Auto) | | | |
| 7. check queue (Ops Mgr) | 15 sec | | |
| 8. check queue (Tech) | 15 sec | | |
| 9. escalate? (Ops Mgr) | 10 min | 3/day | |
| 10. escalate? (Tech) | 10 min | 1/day | |
| 11. assign to Tech | 1 min | | |
| 12. work ticket | 30 min | 6/day | |
| 13. fix and confirm | 10 min | | |
| 14. OK ticket resolved? | | | |
| 15. close | 5 min | | |
| 16. document | 15 min | | |

*There are various "gray areas" in which subjective judgment is required to apply the method. For example, should volume metrics be included on the VSM? In settling this kind of question, you should take whichever approach seems most useful to the team in looking for improvements. Making these judgment calls becomes easier with experience.*

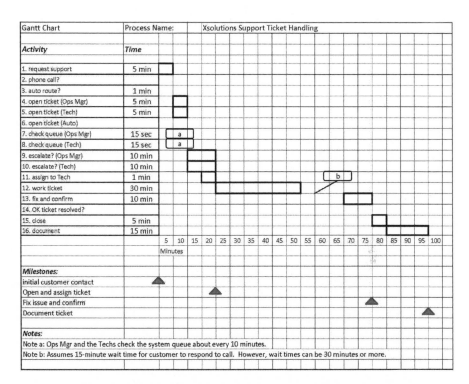

Figure 23. Gantt Chart, Support Ticket Handling Process

The total width of the chart is scaled to represent the typical total duration (cycle time) of the process (including typical wait times). Wait times are indicated on the chart by separations between the end of one bar and the beginning of another, with associated notes placed at the bottom of the chart. Figure 23 shows that the typical cycle time for the XSolutions process is around ninety-five minutes.

After entering horizontal bars for each process activity, the primary "milestones" for the process are identified and positioned along the timeline. These milestones were identified in Step 1. At this point, those milestones can either be accepted or modified based upon observations made during Step 2. For XSolutions, the Step 1 milestones were accepted and noted on the Gantt chart.

The Gantt chart and the milestone points help the team identify the primary process segments. This is useful in later steps as they identify waiting time waste and formulate ways of improving the process by reducing segment durations or cycle times. The milestone points also provide a shorthand way of describing the process on the canvas.

*In the first two steps, you should stay focused on understanding and documenting the current situation. While it is natural to think about possible improvements at this point, it is important to keep an open mind and "park" those ideas until Step 6. This parking will ensure that you don't jump to conclusions about a solution before you really understand the problem.*

Note that there is no Lean Event Canvas entry for Step 2. The deliverable for this step is the value stream map, which consists of the value stream flowchart, the process details table, and the Gantt chart.

*Step 2 Questions:*

1) What activities are necessary to move from the triggering milestone (process start) to the ending milestone (process finish)? Which process actors (identified in Step 1) carry out which activities?

2) What is the sequence of activities? Where are the decision points that cause the process to be carried out in different ways depending upon that decision?

3) How many times per day or per week is this process executed (volume)? Is the process carried out for one work unit or a batch of units? If a batch, how large is the typical batch (e.g., paying a typical batch of 50 invoices)? At what points in the process are these batches of material or information held?

4) What is the typical actual time required to complete each activity for a typical batch of work units (*excluding* any down time or waiting time)? (The answer is often "it depends"—if so, then at least come up with a rough time estimate or a range of times—that is better than not answering the question.)

5) How long does it typically take to get from start to finish in the process (cycle time)? How much of this time is spent in actual work time (activity time), and how much is spent in waiting or downtime? At what points in the process does the waiting occur?

6) Are there any specific process performance metrics that are captured for this process? (If yes, obtain records and history of this data for use in Step 3.)

## Step 3: Assess Value and Process Performance[41]

Value is produced in a process by the activities that transform the inputs into the outputs. It is this transformation that creates the value. Because the value is produced for the benefit of process customers and other process stakeholders, these individuals define what value is. In this case, value is in the eyes of the stakeholder-beholders!

In this step, the team seeks to understand what the process customers perceive as value in terms of "value factors" for process quality and process speed. The process customers are a key source of information about quality because they are the primary users of the process output. Regarding speed, process customers are also quite invested in obtaining the outputs in a timely manner.

In effect, the quality and speed value factors represent the quality of the process outputs (used by the process customers) and the time it takes to produce those outputs. In eliciting these factors, the team should interview the process customers and ask them to be as specific as possible with regard to the meaning of these two value types. Value factors should be sufficiently concrete so that they are either measurable or at least observable.

The team also needs to assess what the organizational agents consider to be the relevant productivity and compliance factors for the target process. Productivity value factors might be defined as labor hours required or distance walked to produce a certain level of output. They might involve materials consumed or space required to carry out the process. It is not necessary to identify every possible type of resource required, only the resources considered critical by the organizational agents.

Compliance value factors may be internally established standards, or they may be set based on the requirements of external organizations,

41    Refer to Chapter 5.

such as the safety standards established by OSHA. Other regulatory and legal standards may apply, especially in the financial services and health care industries.

Once all of the value factors are clearly defined by the process customers and organizational agents, the team then assesses the actual performance of the process using those factors as a measuring stick. As with value factors, this information is obtained from the process stakeholders, supported by process metrics if at all possible.

Organizations often do not have metrics available for the current process because data collection systems usually accumulate revenues, costs, and other data by organizational unit rather than by process or value stream. Therefore, it may be necessary to set up a procedure for capturing relevant process metrics, either before or during the Lean event.

All stakeholders may not agree as to the nature or importance of particular value factors and/or actual performance ratings. For example, different process customers may define quality in different ways, while there may be disagreement among organizational agents regarding the importance of different compliance factors. Rather than trying to reach a consensus, keep track of these differences—they will probably require some tradeoffs to be made during Step 6.

The column-2 Lean Event Canvas entries for the XSolutions event are shown on Figure 24. Note that both column 1 (Figure 21) and column 2 (Figure 24) of the canvas are split into an upper and lower section. Entries to the upper sections are driven by information from process customers about quality and speed while the lower sections are based on feedback from organizational agents about productivity and compliance. Also note how each statement of performance begins with a letter grade that best reflects the perceived rating of process performance for that factor. This is followed by a brief explanation as to why that particular grade was assigned by the team.

Lean Event Canvas for _____

| Value Factors | Performance Grades |
|---|---|
| **Quality:** | **Quality:** |
| Complete resolution of the issue | **A-,** 94% of issues in target process were resolved (exceptions were noted for further study) |
| Confirm resolution with client | **A,** Confirmation is consistently obtained |
| Acknowledge receipt of client request | **C,** Acknowledgments are given but only if the client asks |
| "No hassles" | **A-,** Most clients saw the process as relatively easy |
| No loss of data | **A,** No losses of data were identified |
| **Speed:** | **Speed:** |
| First response within 15 minutes | **A-,** 92% of tickets were responded to within 15 minutes |
| Fix issue within 75 minutes | **B+,** 78% of tickets in the target process were fixed within 75 minutes |

| *Productivity:* | *Productivity:* |
|---|---|
| No. of tickets per labor-hour | **B**, Appears to be excessive time spent in double checking and other actions |
| Contractor expense per ticket | **B**, May be instances where Techs could have addressed the issue without escalating to contractors (40% of tickets were escalated) |
| *Compliance:* | *Compliance:* |
| Maintain data security and privacy | **A**, No known security or privacy breaches |
| Create and complete internal documentation | **C**, Techs sometimes short-cut this activity, some tickets are not closed even after issue is resolved |

Figure 24. Lean Event Canvas Entries for
Column 2 (Step 3): Value, Performance

*Step 3 Questions:*

1) What specific features make up "quality" for the target process in the eyes of process customers? (General statements about customer satisfaction are not sufficient—quality needs to be defined in specific reference to the target process.)

2) What do process customers expect in terms of process "speed"? What do these customers see as critical time intervals (e.g., from what time point to what time point), and how long do customers expect these time intervals to take?

3) Are process customers happy with the current process performance? What aspects are deficient?

4) What do process customers see as the most pressing problems associated with this process?

5) What do process metrics (if available) show in terms of process performance? How does this performance compare with industry standards or corporate benchmarks? What are the time trends in performance?

6) What do the organizational agents consider to be the most important resources to be conserved in this process? (labor hours, cost of supplies, physical space, other resources?) What production metrics are most relevant (e.g., number of transactions completed)? How can the resource and production metrics be combined into a relevant productivity metric (e.g., number of transactions per labor-hour)?

7) What do the organizational agents consider to be important and relevant compliance factors, considering both internal company policies and norms as well as external stakeholder guidelines and regulations?

### Step 4: *Identify Points of Waste and Root Causes*[42]

In this step, the team observes waste and attempts to identify one or more possible root causes. One approach to recognizing waste involves reviewing the activities on the value stream map and then classifying each activity as being either value-producing or waste. Sometimes, the wasteful activities are further broken down into two types: necessary waste and pure waste. Necessary waste activities do not produce value but are difficult to eliminate, while pure waste activities could be more easily eliminated or reduced.

While assessing one activity at a time and distinguishing necessary waste from pure waste can be a useful starting point, it is often difficult to agree on the classification of each activity, especially with regard to whether or not a particular activity is necessary waste or pure waste. Also, waste sometimes results from the interaction of multiple activities; therefore, looking at each activity individually can result in "not seeing the forest for the trees."

Rather than classifying each individual activity in the process as to its waste type, it may be more useful to identify one or more "points of waste" that exist within the process. A point of waste refers to a particular problem area or a pattern of waste that the team recognizes within the process, regardless of whether or not that waste is tied to a single activity or a series of activities.

In identifying points of waste, the team should use the seven classic types of waste as a checklist. These seven types include defects, waiting, excessive levels of production, inventory, walking, processing, and transportation. On the Lean Event Canvas, the team can list the waste points according to the four general waste categories: 1) defects, 2) waiting, 3) overproduction (excessive production and inventory), and 4) non-productive activities (excessive walking, processing, and transportation).

---

42   Refer to Chapter 6.

*Some waste points may relate to multiple waste categories. Listing the point under the "correct category" is really not that important. What is important is identifying the waste in the first place.*

The team should attempt to link the points of waste back to the performance deficiencies ("value gaps") that were identified in Step 3. All deficiencies from Step 3 should be reflected in at least one waste point. Identifying waste may actually reveal some new types of value that were not previously identified. If so, the team should return to Step 3 and add those value definitions to the canvas.

Note that the team does not have to identify an example of every type of waste or even every possible waste. Remember the philosophy of the Lean method is to just go ahead and do it. So, if you don't find the waste the first time, you may find it later on in the event or after the event is finished. The points of waste that were identified in the support ticket handling process are listed on Figure 25.

Once the points of waste are identified, then their possible root causes can be explored. For some points of waste, the root cause may be quite difficult to understand. For others, the root cause may be fairly obvious. So root cause analysis should be used if and when it is useful in better understanding the nature of that point of waste and how that waste might be eliminated.

The primary Lean tool for uncovering the root causes of waste is the 5Whys technique. This technique involves asking "why" the point of waste exists. After suggesting an answer, you then ask why that is true (the second "why"). This process continues for a number of cycles (not necessarily five) until you arrive at an answer (root cause) that can be effectively reduced or eliminated.

| **Defects:** | **Overproduction:** |
|---|---|
| • Not always providing acknowledgment of ticket opening as desired by some clients<br>• Nature of the issue is sometimes misunderstood by the Tech<br>• Documentation screens are sometimes not complete or accurate<br><br>**Waiting:**<br>• Client waiting for ticket resolution (time between step 1 and step 15)<br>• Tech waiting for client to return the call (time between step 13 and step 14) | • Excessive documentation (some fields are not needed)<br><br>**Non-productive Activities:**<br>• Many clicks are required to complete ticket handling activities<br>• Many screens are needed in searching for information<br>• Ops Mgr and all Techs are repeatedly checking the queue for unassigned tickets |

Figure 25. Lean Event Canvas Entries for
Column 3 (Step 4): Points of Waste

As an example, here is a summary of the 5Whys technique as it was applied to the defect: "nature of issue is sometimes misunderstood by the Tech":

---

*1) Why is the nature of a client issue sometimes misunderstood by the Tech?*

The Tech and the client do not communicate effectively.

*2) Why do the Tech and client not communicate effectively?*

In some cases, it is difficult for clients to explain their IT problems. In other cases, the Tech may not know what questions to ask the client.

*3) Why is it difficult for clients to explain their IT problems?*

Clients may be unfamiliar with relevant IT concepts and terminology.

*4) Why are clients sometimes unfamiliar with relevant IT concepts and terminology?*

Clients may lack training and/or experience with these concepts and terms.

*5) Why do Techs not know what questions to ask the client?*

Techs may lack training and/or experience with the particular type of issue being presented by the client.

---

The series of why questions was terminated at this point because they were pointing toward a solution that involved training the Techs and perhaps even providing guidance to the clients.

*Step 4 Questions:*

1) In reviewing the "value gaps" in column 2 of the canvas (lowest grades), what types of waste seem to be contributing to these deficiencies?

2) What types of defects can be observed? Defects include activities that must be redone and/or the production of outputs that do not satisfy process customer needs.

3) How much waiting is involved in the process, and at what points in the process does this waiting occur?

4) Is there evidence of overproduction (e.g., producing too much material or information, excessive inventories of material or information)?

5) What are the non-productive activities in terms of excessive walking, transportation, and/or processing? Note that this requires subjective judgment, perhaps based on the intuition that the process could be carried out more efficiently (even if the exact means for doing so is not clearly understood).

6) For each point of waste identified, why are these wastes being produced? What are the possible root causes for these waste points?

### Step 5: Formulate a Lean Vision[43]

After recognizing the points of waste and their root causes in Step 4, it is now possible to create a future vision or "Lean vision." This Lean vision is an image of the process with little or no waste and with a smooth flow pattern. In essence, this requires that an "ideal" process be imagined. This image should stretch the imagination by eliminating most of the waste, although it should do so in a realistic way.

At the time the team creates the Lean vision, you will probably not know exactly how it might be achieved. This is appropriate because the vision is meant to be something to work toward rather than a specific plan of action. Remember that the learning cycle of the Lean method continues after the end of the current event and is a never-ending pursuit of incremental improvement. The future vision may even change with time, but you need to start somewhere.

Sometimes it is helpful to draw out the Lean vision in the form of a "future value stream map." This future map is abstract and simplified and does not include all of the details in the value stream flowchart and Gantt chart. Rather, it is a rough vision of what the process could possibly look like in the future. Creating a physical chart helps the whole team participate in creating and evaluating the vision.

Another useful technique in imagining a future Lean vision is to calculate the *value-added time percentage*. This metric represents the percentage of the total cycle time that involves some type of value-producing activity. In assessing a target process, it is common to find that a very small percentage of the total cycle time is actually used for producing value while the rest of the time is taken up in waiting or producing other types of waste. In your Lean vision, try to imagine a process in which 90 or 100 percent of the cycle time is used to produce value!

---

43    Refer to Chapter 7, Lean Vision.

For the XSolutions support ticket handling process, a Lean vision statement was developed and is presented below (refer to Figure 26):

> In our Lean vision of this process, most issues are re-
> solved by XSolutions even before they are identified by
> the client (using preventative measures). Of the issues
> that are reported by clients, 80 percent are resolved with-
> in 5 minutes and 95 percent are resolved within 15 min-
> utes.

## Step 6: Evaluate and Select Improvements[44]

Finding an improvement is essentially a creative design activity. In this activity, there are usually a number of iterations through a cycle until it is determined that the design work is finished and a decision can be made to accept and implement the chosen improvement. This creative process can be described as an iterative cycle of three activities which include envisioning, experimenting, and evaluating.

### Envision

Using observations and assessments of the current situation as a base of reference, possible improvement actions are suggested. This part of the step should begin with a consideration of the Lean vision that was formulated in Step 5 and the root causes of the waste points that were identified in Step 4. These root causes are essentially controllable factors that lead to the waste and, therefore, are a logical starting point for identifying solutions. The list of improvement types and common Lean solutions described in Chapter 7 can be used to trigger ideas.

### Experiment

The most promising actions envisioned are subjected to an "experiment." This experiment might be an actual trial attempt at implementing and testing the action. Alternatively, it may consist of a "thought experiment" in which the change is imagined with regard to what is likely to occur if that change were implemented.

### Evaluate

Based on the experiment, the action under consideration is evaluated for its potential or actual influence on reducing the waste points identified in Step 4 and closing the value gaps identified in Step 3. The team may decide the improvements are sufficient so it is time to move on to

---

44   Refer to Chapter 7, Flow as the Solution and Improvement Cycle.

Step 7. Alternatively, the team may believe further consideration is warranted; therefore, a revised or new type of improvement is envisioned and the above tasks are repeated. However, do not fall into the trap of getting caught up in too much analysis and/or lengthy discussions of alternatives.

A particular solution will have different effects on different value factors, and there may be tradeoffs in terms of different types of wastes. For example, an action may improve quality and reduce speed, but it may also lead to an increase in cost. In addition, the importance of each value factor may vary for different stakeholders, and there may be tradeoffs to consider in this regard as well.

Some Lean practitioners believe that only one improvement action should be implemented at a time. This approach allows for the effect of that single improvement to be clearly assessed. If multiple improvements are implemented simultaneously, then the actual effect of each individual action cannot be clearly determined. However, because of the effort associated with carrying out a kaizen event, these events usually result in a number of improvement actions.

The step ends when the kaizen team decides that a list of worthwhile improvement actions has been identified. The list is a deliverable of Step 6, and it is used as the basis for completing Step 7. The list of solutions selected for XSolutions is shown below:

- Add an acknowledgment step after the ticket is opened
- Remove unnecessary fields from the documentation template
- Develop a work assignment and tracking system that reduces the need for frequent checking of the queue
- Develop and train Techs on rules for diagnosing problems and making escalation decisions
- Develop an integrated system that facilitates single click searches

*Step 6 Questions:*

1) What can we do to move in the direction of the Lean vision?

2) What types of work assignment changes might be useful (e.g., work-load balancing)?

3) What types of layouts or facility designs might be useful (e.g., application of 5S technique, work cells)?

4) What types of procedural or method changes might be useful (e.g., batch size reduction, kitting)?

5) Can changes to activity sequence be helpful (e.g., shifting activities from sequential to parallel)?

6) What types of tools, equipment, and/or IT solutions might be useful (e.g., kanban system, kanban board, poka-yoke tool)?

### Step 7: Standardize the Improvements[45]

This step involves finalizing and standardizing the improvement actions selected in the previous step and preparing to move forward with maintaining those changes on an on-going basis as process associates continue to search for further improvements.

Any improvements that can be implemented within the time constraints of the Lean event should be completed immediately. These are listed on the Lean Event Canvas as "Immediate Actions." Improvements that cannot be completed during the event are either scheduled for completion with an associated implementation plan ("Scheduled Actions") or they are designated as "Future Possible Actions" if they require further study and consideration.

As noted on Figure 26, the immediate actions that were taken as part of the XSolutions event included adding an acknowledgment step and removing unnecessary fields from the documentation template. Actions scheduled for implementation included the development of a work assignment and tracking system as well as rules for diagnosing problems and making escalation decisions. (An implementation plan for completing these two actions was agreed upon.) The development of an integrated search system was considered to be a future possible action because the design of such a system would require considerable time and cost and the potential benefits did not clearly justify this effort.

The immediate improvements are validated and become part of the regular work activity. This involves creating and/or updating the standard work guide, setting up appropriate visual controls, and training all relevant process actors who were not part of the kaizen team.

A standard work guide is a clear presentation of the process procedures and is made accessible to all process actors. It can take various forms

---

45    Refer to Chapter 4, Standard Work and Visual Controls.

ranging from checklists to videos. (Refer to Chapter 4 for sample formats.) The standard work guide for the XSolutions process is shown on Figure 27. This is a "desktop procedure" format that is intended to be a quick reference for process actors without specifying every detail of the process.

| **Lean Vision:** | **Scheduled Actions:** |
|---|---|
| In our Lean vision of this process, most issues are resolved by XSolutions even before they are identified by the client (using preventative measures). Of the issues reported by clients, 80 percent are resolved within 5 minutes and 95 percent are resolved within 15 minutes. | • Develop a work assignment and tracking system that reduces the need for frequent checking of the queue<br>• Develop and train Techs on rules for diagnosing problems and making escalation decisions |
| **Immediate Actions** | **Future Possible Actions:** |
| • Add an acknowledgment step after the ticket is opened<br>• Remove unnecessary fields from the documentation template | • Develop an integrated system that facilitates for single click searches |

Figure 26. Lean Event Canvas Entries for
Column 4 (Steps 5, 6, and 7): Vision, Improvements

Visual controls should be relatively simple, focused, and highly visible and accessible to the process actors. These controls should include at least one "tracking metric." This metric is selected or created in order to track the most important performance gain expected from implementing the selected improvement. The tracking metric is useful in determining the extent to which the improvement is having the expected effect. A lack of response in the tracking metric indicates that the action is not effective and that other improvements should be considered.

---

### XSolutions Support Ticket Handling Process
### Standard Work Guide for Techs

1) Client requests support

2) Open ticket and send acknowledgment to client
*Goal: within 10 minutes from client's support request*
    -> Use email template "Support Ticket Acknowledgment Email"

3) Triage the ticket and make escalation decision
    -> Follow "Support Ticket Escalation Rules"

4) Work the ticket
    -> Use Ticket Support system

5) Fix the issue and call or email the client to confirm the fix
*Goal: within 45 minutes of opening the ticket*

6) Document the ticket
    -> Use Ticket Documentation screen
*Goal: document all tickets by the end of the day*

Figure 27. Standard Work Guide for
Support Ticket Handling Process

It is often the case that the most appropriate tracking metric is not currently available. In this case, it is important that the team create a system for capturing and tracking the metric. This type of system might start out as a simple handwritten worksheet that can eventually be automated.

For XSolutions, the tracking metrics that were selected included the cycle time and the percentage of tickets that were escalated. The XSolutions team defined "cycle time" as the time interval between request for support (Step 1) and fixing the issue (Step 13). The visual control that incorporated these metrics was a daily run chart similar to the one shown in Figure 28. The data for this chart was initially captured on a paper worksheet that was prepared and used to record and observe the relevant values for each day (see Figure 29). This data was subsequently captured directly from the ticket tracking system, and online run chart reports were automatically generated on a real-time basis. These reports were made available to both local and remote Techs.

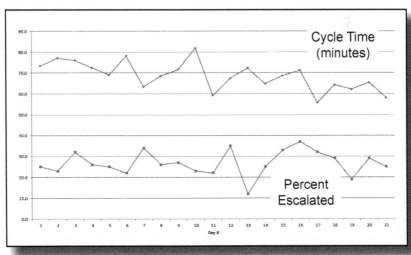

Figure 28. Run Chart for Tracking Metrics

TRACKING METRIC WORKSHEET
SUPPORT TICKET HANDLING

For Requests Received on: __WED  5/18/16__ (day/date)

| | Col 1 | Col 2 | Col 3 | Col 4 | Col 5 |
|---|---|---|---|---|---|
| | Ticket # | Time support request was received from client | Escalated? | Time that fix was confirmed with client | Total minutes (from Col 2 to Col 4) |
| 1 | 207 | 9:05 AM | ✓ | 9:37 AM | 32 |
| 2 | 208 | 9:12 | ✓ | 10:31 | 79 |
| 3 | 210 | 9:15 | YES | ✓ | ✓ |
| 4 | 211 | 9:45 | YES | ✓ | ✓ |
| 5 | 212 | 10:32 | ✓ | 10:52 | 20 |
| 6 | 214 | 11:51 | ✓ | 1:43 PM | 112 |
| 7 | 216 | 1:12 PM | ✓ | 2:50 | 98 |
| 8 | 217 | 2:28 | YES | ✓ | ✓ |
| 9 | 220 | 3:10 | ✓ | 4:12 | 62 |
| 10 | 221 | 5:40 | ✓ | 6:31 | 51 |
| 11 | 225 | 8:52 | ✓ | 10:40 | 108 |
| 12 | 226 | 11:28 | ✓ | 1:06 AM | 98 |
| 13 | | | | | |
| 14 | | | | | |
| 15 | | | | | |
| 16 | | | | | |
| 17 | | | | | |
| 18 | | | | | |
| 19 | | | | | |
| 20 | | | | | |

Number of tickets opened: **12**
Percent of tickets escalated: **25%**
Average process cycle time: (MINUTES) **73.3**

Figure 29. Tracking Metric Worksheet for
Support Ticket Handling Process

*Step 7 Questions:*

1) Which of the selected improvement actions can be implemented immediately as part of this event?

2) For the immediate actions, what key aspects of the improved process need to be documented as standard work? How can these aspects best be documented in a way accessible to process actors?

3) What tracking metric(s) would be most useful in assessing the effectiveness of the immediate improvements? How can this metric be captured, tracked, and reported?

4) What kind of visual controls would help to sustain and build on the improvements? Where should these controls be placed? Can the tracking metrics (from question 3) be incorporated into the visual control?

5) Among the selected actions that cannot be implemented immediately, which will be scheduled for implementation and which will be held for further consideration?

6) For scheduled improvement actions, what further steps are needed, who is responsible for these steps, and what is the schedule for their completion?

# Chapter 13

# Continuing the Journey

IN THIS CHAPTER, I provide some relevant readings to help readers who are not in manufacturing to continue with their Lean journey. These books are some of my favorites, especially for executive and entrepreneurial readers.[46] However, I realize this is an incomplete list, and I extend my apologies to the many other authors who could have been listed.

Two of the most prominent books that describe Lean and the Toyota Production System are *Lean Thinking* (Womack and Jones 2003) and *The Toyota Way* (Liker 2004). Although strongly influenced by manufacturing applications and examples, these two books provide a full overview of Lean concepts and practices. The authors of both books describe their own models of Lean. The Womack and Jones book emphasizes the five Lean principles of Value, Value Stream, Flow, Pull, and Perfection, while the Liker book presents a 4P model that includes Philosophy, Process, People/Partners, and Problem Solving. Liker and Ross (2017) have just released an updated version of the 4P model with special emphasis on service applications in their book entitled *The Toyota Way to Service Excellence*.

---

46    Refer to the Bibliography section of this book for full titles and citations for these readings.

A more recent Lean book that is focused on executive-level readers is *The Lean CEO* by Jacob Stoller (2015). This book presents the story of Lean in a case study format as told by twenty-eight leaders from various organizations and industries. Readers in health care will find useful cases and insights in Chapter 12, while those in government should be interested in reading Chapter 13 to learn about recent Lean efforts in Canada and in the U.S. states of Washington and Connecticut.

Books that especially focus on the Lean method and surface culture components of the Lean system include *Lean Production Simplified* (Dennis 2016), *Creating a Lean Culture* (Mann 2010), and *Toyota Kata* (Rother 2010). Dennis' book offers an in-depth, practical look at many of the most important Lean tools and techniques. The book by David Mann provides an extensive discussion of surface culture practices, including many detailed examples and useful forms. Rother's book provides unique insight and hands-on methods for understanding and acquiring the habits of practical scientific thinking.

The deep culture component of the Lean system is addressed in the *Toyota Way* (Liker 2004) by recognizing that "Respect for People" is one of the two foundational pillars of the Toyota Way (with the other pillar being "Continuous Improvement"). Books not specifically written on the topic of Lean management but that describe and explain the importance of culture, respect, and trust in organizations include *Joy, Inc.* (Sheridan 2013), *Carrots and Sticks Don't Work* (Marciano 2010), *The Respect Effect* (Meshanko 2013), and *The Speed of Trust* (Covey 2006).

Useful online resources for newsletters, training, and certification programs include:

- American Society for Quality (2016), www.asq.org
- Association for Manufacturing Excellence (2016), www.ame.org
- Lean Enterprise Institute (2016), www.lean.org
- SME (2016), www.sme.org/lean-certification.aspx
- The Essence of Lean (2017), www.essenceoflean.com

Good luck on your journey. I wish you the best!

# BIBLIOGRAPHY

American Society for Quality (2016). http://asq.org/cert/six-sigma-black-belt.

Association for Manufacturing Excellence (2016). http://www.ame.org/.

Chakravorty, Satya S. (2010). "Where process-improvement projects go wrong." *Wall Street Journal*, January 25, 2010.

Collins, Jim (2001). *Good to Great: Why Some Companies Make the Leap...And Others Don't.* Harper Business, New York, NY.

Covey, Stephen R. (1989). *The 7 Habits of Highly Effective People: Powerful Lessons In Personal Change.* Simon and Schuster, New York, NY.

Covey, Stephen M.R. (2006). *The Speed of Trust: The One Thing That Changes Everything.* Free Press, New York, NY.

Dennis, Pascal (2016). *Lean Production Simplified: A Plain-Language Guide to the World's Most Powerful Production System.* Third edition. Productivity Press, New York, NY.

Dinero, Donald (2005). *Training Within Industry: The Foundation of Lean.* Productivity Press, New York, NY.

Duncan, Ewan and Ritter, Ron (2014). "Next frontiers for Lean." *McKinsey Quarterly*, February 2014.

Fitzsimmons, James, Fitzsimmons, Mona and Bordoloi, Sanjeev (2014). *Service Management: Operations, Strategy, Information Technology.* Irwin/McGraw-Hill, New York, NY.

Fleming, John H. (2007). *Human Sigma: Managing the Employee-Customer Encounter.* Gallup Press, New York, NY.

Imai, Masaaki (1986). *Kaizen: The Key to Japan's Competitive Success.* McGraw-Hill, New York, NY.

Koltko-Rivera, Mark E. (2004). "The psychology of worldviews." *Review of General Psychology*, 8(1), 3-58.

Lean. (2016, June 19). In *Wikipedia, The Free Encyclopedia.* Retrieved 22:03, April 1, 2016, from https://en.wikipedia.org/w/index.php?title=Lean&oldid=696984578

Lean Enterprise Institute (2016). http://www.lean.org/.

Liker, Jeffrey K. (2004). *The Toyota Way: 14 Management Principles From the World's Greatest Manufacturer.* McGraw-Hill, New York, NY.

Liker, Jeffrey K. and Ross, Karyn (2017). *The Toyota Way to Service Excellence: Lean Transformation In Service Organizations.* McGraw-Hill, New York, NY.

Mann, David (2010). *Creating a lean culture: Tools to sustain lean conversions.* Productivity Press, New York, NY.

Marciano, Paul L. (2010). *Carrots and Sticks Don't Work: Build a Culture of Employee Engagement With the Principles of RESPECT.* McGraw-Hill, New York, NY.

McDonnell, Dan and Locher, Drew A. (2013). *Unleashing the Power of 3P: The Key to Breakthrough Improvement.* Taylor and Francis Group, Boca Raton, Florida.

McGregor, D.M. (1960). *The Human Side of Enterprise*. McGraw-Hill, New York, NY.

Meshanko, Paul (2013). *The Respect Effect: Using the Science of Neuro-leadership to Inspire a More Loyal and Productive Workplace*. McGraw-Hill, New York, NY.

Pande, Peter S., Neuman, Robert P. and Cavanagh, Roland R. (2000). *The Six Sigma Way: How GE, Motorola and Other Top Companies Are Honing Their Performance*. McGraw-Hill, New York, NY.

Pink, Daniel H. (2009). *Drive: The Surprising Truth About What Motivates Us*. Penguin Group, New York, NY.

Polanyi, M. (1966). *The Tacit Dimension*. London, Routledge & Kegan Paul.

Ries, Eric (2011). *The Lean Startup: How Today's Entrepreneurs Use Continuous Innovation to Create Radically Successful Businesses*. Crown Business. New York, NY.

Rother, Mike and Shook, John (1999). *Learning to See: Value Stream Mapping to Create Value and Eliminate Muda*. Lean Enterprise Institute, Cambridge, MA.

Rother, Mike (2010). *Toyota Kata: Managing People For Improvement, Adaptiveness, and Superior Results*. McGraw-Hill, New York, NY.

Schein, Edgar H. (2010). *Organizational Culture and Leadership*, 4th edition. John Wiley & Sons, Hoboken, NJ.

Schmenner, R. W. (2004). "Service businesses and productivity." *Decision Sciences*, 35(3), 333-347.

Sheridan, Richard (2013). *Joy Inc: How We Built a Workplace People Love*. Penguin Group, New York, NY.

SMART criteria. (2016, April 1). In *Wikipedia, The Free Encyclopedia.* Retrieved 04:59, April 2, 2016, from https://en.wikipedia.org/w/index.php?title=SMART_criteria&oldid=712986298

SME (2016). http://www.sme.org/lean-certification.aspx.

Stoller, Jacob (2015). *The Lean CEO: Building World-Class Organizations One Step at a Time.* McGraw-Hill, New York, NY.

Sutherland, Jeff (2014). *Scrum: The Art of Doing Twice the Work In Half the Time.* Crown Business, New York, NY.

Womack, James P. and Jones, Daniel T. (2003). *Lean Thinking: Banish Waste and Create Wealth In Your Corporation.* Simon & Schuster, New York, NY.

# INDEX

Made in the USA
Columbia, SC
16 December 2020